DATE DUE

APR 1 8 1984			
MAY 8 1984			
APR 1 4 1986			
MAR 1 6 1988			
APR 1 8 1988			
DEC 21 1989			
SEP 2 8 1990			
OCT 2 1 199			
JUN 8 1994			
APR 2 2 2000			
NOV 2 5 2008			

THE BEST IDEAS IN THE WORLD ARE FREE

AT YOUR

FORM 48 5/64   **NEW HAVEN PUBLIC LIBRARY**

TINTORETTO

PHAIDON

IACOBVS·TENTORETVS·PICT·VENT^{OR·}^{IVS·}

IPSIVS·F·

SELF-PORTRAIT OF TINTORETTO. 1588. Paris, Louvre. ⟨24 X 20⟩

TINTORETTO

(Jacopo Robusti) m.j.

THE PAINTINGS AND DRAWINGS

WITH THREE HUNDRED ILLUSTRATIONS

BY HANS TIETZE

7B
T495
G

PHAIDON PUBLISHERS INC.

DISTRIBUTED BY THE OXFORD UNIVERSITY PRESS

NEW YORK · MCMXLVIII

MADE IN AUSTRIA
PRINTED BY WAGNER'SCHE UNIV.-BUCHDRUCKEREI GES. M. B. H., INNSBRUCK

FOREWORD

T HE present volume, although planned on slightly different lines, is the natural sequence to my book on Titian, published by the Phaidon Press in 1935. In each case an incentive to write the book was given by an exhibition held in the Palazzo Pesaro in Venice shortly before the publication. The "Mostra del Tintoretto" in 1937—like that of Titian which preceded it by two years—not only brought together under the most favourable conditions a selection of the most important works, but also—and this is the essential point— surrounded the personality of the artist to whom it was dedicated with an atmosphere of veneration which was bound to provide an incentive for new literary studies of his work. A large number of people for whom Tintoretto was little more than a name were able to appreciate his greatness and his vitality with their own eyes. To achieve the same result with the aid of words and pictures is the aim of my book.

This is more necessary in Tintoretto's case than it is with certain other artists, the recognition and admiration of whom form a part of universal culture. Tintoretto lived at a time when the feeling that a zenith in the development of art had just been passed was becoming a firm conviction. The critical attitude with which, despite the loud admiration of many, his achievements were received, persisted to an exaggerated degree throughout the periods which followed. Writers on Tintoretto, even if they did not pass definitely unfavour- able judgement on him, were unable to refrain from adopting a somewhat apologetic attitude. An incentive was thus lacking which encouraged the investigation of the lives of other artists, handed down to us under happier auspices. To what a great extent real affection is a help to understanding is proved by Ruskin's and still more by Thode's writings on Tintoretto, in which the intimate understanding of his artistic personality paved the way for their critical studies. Thode's monograph on Tintoretto—together with the numerous critical studies supplementing it which he published in the *Repertorium für Kunstwissenschaft*—has remained the fundamental work for the understanding and study of Tintoretto.

Succeeding generations developed these fundamental notions in various directions. While Osmaston in England and F. Fosca in France sought to enlarge our general knowledge of the artist by increasing and deepening our knowledge of details, in Italy Mary Pittaluga and in Germany von der Bercken and Mayer, as well as Detlev Freiherr von Hadeln, have made successful investigations into various aspects of his activity, enriching his *œuvre* by a series of valuable attributions. Bercken-Mayer and Pittaluga have also given comprehensive descriptions of the results of their various studies. Hadeln was prevented by his premature death from crowning his life's work in this way, as he too had planned to do. That his studies on Tintoretto should thus remain fragmentary undoubtedly deprives the history of art of a valuable contribution; for Hadeln's scattered articles on various pertinent questions reveal such a thorough mastery of the vast amount of material that we have every reason to feel that we have been deprived of valuable conclusions concerning Tintoretto as a painter. Nevertheless it is a consolation that Hadeln, in his book and in numerous articles on Tintoretto's drawings, has given us his final conclusions on this section of his work, conclusions from which no later investigator has deviated without serious detriment to Scholarship. That these achievements of Hadeln can stand the amplifications which in many respects they need will be proved by the scientific catalogue of sixteenth-century Venetian drawings which I have prepared in collaboration with E. Tietze-Conrat. Only in this way shall I be able to repay in full the debt which, even in the compilation of a modest monograph like the present, I feel I owe to the great scholar who has passed away.

In conformity with the rules of literary courtesy I wish here to express my thanks to the directors of museums and collectors who made my task easier, and to those persons who have placed material for reproduction at my disposal, especially Messrs. Barbantini, Lorenzetti and Moschini in Venice, E. G. Thompson in London, F. Thompson at Chatsworth, and Lord Duveen of Millbank in New York. I also remember with particular gratitude the valuable help I have received from Sir Robert Witt's incomparable Library in London.

London 1939   H. TIETZE

THE outbreak of the war prevented the publication of the book which was practically ready in 1939, so much so that in publishing it now we are forced to retain its text and illustrations as they were then established. Not only has our book on the "Drawings of the Venetian painters" including Tintoretto's since been published (New York 1944) but further studies by ourselves and others resulted in various deviations from earlier opinions and rectifications of errors. Radical alterations however being impossible, I had to content myself with bringing the notes up to date and with adding a few illustrations of paintings which came to my attention during these last years. They hardly modify my conception of Tintoretto's figure of an artist as laid down in the original text of this book.

New York 1947   H. T.

CONTENTS

THE LIFE AND WORK OF TINTORETTO

I

STYLISTIC FEATURES

IT SEEMS inevitable that the figure of Tintoretto should be regarded as overshadowed by the glory of Titian. It is difficult not only for our own generation, which has had the advantage of seeing the works of each of these artists at the Venetian exhibitions of 1935 and 1937 against an incomparable background which will probably never be surpassed, to separate the younger artist from that atmosphere which the elder impregnated with his artistic vitality; previous generations, too, have always felt themselves constrained to measure the greatness of Tintoretto by the standard of Titian.

Titian was the perfector and the perfected. The harmony between his personality and the epoch which formed him, and which he helped to form, lends additional force to the esteem he enjoyed at the time and subsequently. His career was the obvious incarnation of the High Renaissance, which, despite all the objections that may be made against it, has succeeded in retaining its special place in the intellectual history of Europe; his exceptionally long life enabled Titian to take part both in the beginnings and in the zenith of the movement, and the lonely self-fulfilment of the old artist was the sunset glow of the historic transformation which had taken place in the intellectual life of the world. The dramatic rise of this curve heightens the power of a personality to which its harmony with a great historical process gives the pleasing appearance of a natural event.

Very different was the dominating note of Tintoretto's life. When he was born, Titian had with his Assunta just created one of the representative works of the High Renaissance; when he began his activity as a young painter, the curve of its development was just beginning to fall; and when he rose to full dominion over Venetian art, the Renaissance was only a glittering mask, behind which other forms of intellectual culture had achieved their consummation. It was inevitable that he should be looked upon as a decadent. The first writers who mention him mingle criticism with their words. In his Dialogue on Painting, written in 1557, its aim being the glorification of Titian, Dolce, without actually mentioning Tintoretto's name, finds fault with his painting of the Excommunication of Barbarossa in the Sala del Gran Consiglio, because it departs from Titian's principles; and Guisconi in his book on the sights of Venice, published a year before, qualifies his praise of the picture by

a warning against the dangers of hastiness, the same criticism which Aretino
felt it his duty to express in his letters to Tintoretto of a few years before.
The voices which greeted the appearance of the young Titian had had a pleas-
anter and more positive ring; the writers about the middle of the century must
have been aware that Tintoretto was turning away from a form of artistic
expression whose claims to be regarded as classical were derived from the great
talents of its creators and exponents. All the objections which later critics,
with an asperity which can only be explained as due to their instinctive consciousness of the greatness of the man they were attacking, thought fit to
bring up against Tintoretto, and which sometimes make difficult our pure
enjoyment of his artistic personality, such as Titian's harmony affords us,
amount to nothing more than this, that he deviated from the norm which they
considered golden. In other words they objected to the expansion of individual
aspirations towards mannerism and the artistic formation of new needs of
expression, which were Tintoretto's contributions to the rise of Baroque art.

If it is correct to say that every artist more or less portrays himself in
the figures he creates, then the portraits of Titian and Tintoretto ought to
reveal clearly the contrasts between their creators; and this comparison is all
the more instructive because we have good proof of the relationship of pupil
and teacher which existed in this particular field. Even the oldest biographers
of Tintoretto note that his early portraits are so similar to Titian's as to render
confusion likely; later writers have experienced the difficulty of distinguishing
them and have committed considerable errors of attribution, as my own
books on Titian and Tintoretto themselves certainly serve to prove. Nevertheless there is a sharp contrast in their conceptions of portraiture. For
Titian, the individual whom he was painting was a piece of the same natural
vitality which fills every existence; when he portrays them, the penetrating
analysis of their individuality comprises at the same time the historical and
social forces which magnify and enrich their appearances. For Tintoretto the
individual did not have the same attraction as for Titian, nor did he share
Titian's pleasure and gift for extracting every secret from his sitters; Tintoretto
perceived only the purely human elements, while the external appearance never
received from him, the painter of the spiritual, such loving attention as it did
from Titian. The latter painted Emperors and Popes, soldiers and men of
letters, but at the same time he painted men with their contradictions and their
individual destinies. Tintoretto's portraits are simpler, one might almost say
more universal; they are satisfied with an average standard which the master
emphasizes by limiting himself to a few types and by the avoidance of all
deliberate poses and accessories which divert the attention. Whereas Titian
combines the typical with the individual, Tintoretto seeks the individual in the
typical, for which reason his portraits do not create so deep an impression as
Titian's, and despite their high artistic quality remain more colourless and
Frontispiece apathetic. The fact that in his own self-portrait now in the Louvre he for
once abandoned his usual restraint, and gave himself free rein as a portrayer

of great visionary strength, confers upon this picture an exceptional position. Compared with it, Titian's self-portraits fade away into mere descriptions.

It is clear that in his art Tintoretto pursued a different aim from Titian's. The fact that they belonged to successive generations is not a sufficient explanation of this; there is the additional fact that they were essentially different in their social and general intellectual natures. Titian was the son of a peasant and remained a peasant to the end, though he rose to be the painter of the great and of kings, whose equal he felt himself in his heart to be; Tintoretto was a child of the city of Venice and rose to fame in the service of the burghers and their charitable organizations. Titian was filled with such natural force that it flowed from his hand into every picture, and every touch of colour which he gave was in itself rich and beneficent; Tintoretto was not nearly so direct, more sicklied o'er with the pale cast of thought, or, if we are to follow Schiller's differentiation, sentimental as compared with Titian's divine naïveté. Tintoretto's individual creations possess no innate values in themselves, and his colouring, the further he moves away from the early influence of Titian, is subjected to a dominant principle of another kind, namely to light. Might one not perhaps say that for Titian painting was the interpretation of the world through colour, which for him was a natural and normal element of life, while for Tintoretto—notwithstanding his more passionate temperament and more conscious manipulation of all the possibilities of art—it was a freely chosen means of spiritual expression?

Both artists must have been aware of the antitheses which existed between them. The older writers narrate many such cases of tension—sometimes degenerating into petty spite—and later, when we come to discuss the development of Tintoretto's career, we shall have occasion to speak of the measure in which the influence of Titian served him as a starting-point. Here we will only remark that this influence served a double purpose in Tintoretto's artistic development, as a premiss and as an opposing force. We shall insist more strongly than other recent writers have done on the fact that Titian was really Tintoretto's teacher. Despite this Tintoretto—like his contemporary Paolo Veronese, who grew up in such different circumstances, and with whom in the last quarter of the century he shared the sovereignty of Venetian art—set himself in strict opposition to the old master, who had taught both the younger artists the glory of colour.

In reaction against Titian's disintegration of form, which increased as he grew older, both emphasized the importance of form; both understood—as the Venetian art historian Zanetti expressed it as early as the eighteenth century—that it was impossible to go further along this road. When we contemplate the dreamlike visions of Titian's last works, we can understand very well that they must have produced on the painters who came after him the impression of a highly personal achievement and a disinclination to follow the master into the domain of what could no longer be learned or imitated. And in addition to that we must not forget that this problem, besides its more or less

New attitude to form

personal side, had another side which may be said to have had its origin in the history of the world at that time. The Cinquecento played a particularly important part in the formation of a national Italian civilization; it replaced the then prevalent local and provincial development by a national unity which was strong enough to achieve power and recognition as something purely Italian even in other countries. In the field of the formative arts this unity, which formed the substructure of aesthetic programmes and relationships between schools, had as its premiss and consequence an exchange of ideas between Central and Northern Italy. Modern scholarship has emphasized the decisively important contributions which Venetian colouring made to the development of early Baroque in Florence and Rome; parallel with this, North Italian painting—and above all the Venetian school, with which we are here mainly concerned—drew inspiration for its further development from the problems of form in Central Italian painting.

Contemporary theoreticians—and many later critics who were influenced by them — have simplified the difference between the artistic problems of the two regions into a mere primitive opposition between form and colour, maintaining that all the elements necessary for the elimination of the dissension, both in the practice and in the theory of art, were in the air. In many ways the reconciliation actually took place; as regards Tintoretto in particular, at

„Michelangelo's draughtsmanship and Titian's colour"

an early date the formula had already been coined: "Michelangelo's draughtsmanship and Titian's colour." This was supposed to represent the most concise definition of his artistic ambitions; and Ridolfi even maintained that the words could be read on the wall of Tintoretto's studio, like a monumental slogan.

Ridolfi wrote in the middle of the seventeenth century and it is not very difficult to prove that he and his contemporaries compressed into anecdotal form vague traditions and misunderstood utterances of Tintoretto. The slogan itself in its epigrammatic phrasing is found as early as 1548 in the writings of a Venetian art historian without any reference to Tintoretto; and if anybody tried to put it into practice, it was Sebastiano del Piombo, that Venetian who had emigrated to Rome. Tintoretto's remarks on the importance of Florentine draughtsmanship and Titianesque colouring, which were perhaps communicated by letter to his contemporary Borghini, are a kind of acknowledgement to those who influenced his training and to whom he felt he owed a debt, but they do not in any way represent an eclectic programme. He did not aim at the fusion of those contrasting merits the possession of which had raised the two masters mentioned as his models to solitary peaks of eminence. It is, however, completely wrong to imagine Tintoretto as guided by this double star from the very beginning and to think that even in his youthful period he was striving to achieve a synthesis out of antagonistic elements. At that time he merely began deliberately to supplement his training in the school of Titian by the study of Michelangelo's form.

The chief argument brought forward in support of Tintoretto's interest in plastic form has always been his drawings after antique sculptures and after

works by Michelangelo and Gianbologna, and these have also been held to be the *Fig. 137*
chief means by which he achieved mastery of it. That he studied such models
with indefatigable zeal has been recorded by his biographers and confirmed by
the large number of drawings of this kind which have been preserved. But these
drawings—as Hadeln once wrote—are not the relics of a young art student's
course in plaster-work, but the fruits of a master's labours spread over several
decades. In fact they seem less characteristic of his early period than of his
later years. The statues which his oldest biographer, Raffaele Borghini, mentions
as his favourites—Jacopo Sansovino's Mercury and Neptune on the Scala dei
Giganti in the Ducal Palace—were not completed and erected until 1567, while
Michelangelo's figures in the Medici chapel, whose plastic beauty fascinated
Tintoretto almost more than any other work, can only have been familiar to
him from 1557 on in Daniele da Volterra's reproductions. Gianbologna's
works Tintoretto studied only in his old age; this is definitely stated by Borghini and confirmed by the fact that reminiscences of these works occur only in
his late works. Both the Vienna Flagellation, the principal figure in which *Fig. 243*
is derived from Bologna's terracotta relief in Berlin, and the Massacre of the
Innocents on the ground-floor of the Scuola di San Rocco, the composition of *Fig. 258*
which was inspired by Bologna's Rape of the Sabines, belong to Tintoretto's
last period of activity. But while this plastic element remained prominent in
his works until the end, the converse is also true, namely that the striving after
impressiveness in the single figures is also to be found in the masterpiece of his
younger days, the Miracle of St. Mark painted in 1548. In fact this new
phenomenon caused a sensation when the picture was first shown and provoked
violent hostility, among the opponents being Titian, as we learn from a passage
in Aretino's letters. Whether this was due to direct contact with the art of
Michelangelo, or whether other circumstances brought the young Tintoretto face
to face with this problem, is a question which we shall discuss later when
dealing with his development; here it will be sufficient to say that a striving
after plastic effect, surpassing that of Titian, is an inseparable part of Tintoretto's art. The latter achieves its full maturity only when this element becomes
clearly perceptible. Everything he painted before is preparation. To define it
clearly, we must try to determine to what extent the slogan: " Michelangelo's
draughtsmanship and Titian's colour " is applicable to Tintoretto's own share in
the artistic development of his time.

    Draughtsmanship and colouring are technical conceptions. But the language *Draughtsmanship*
of Renaissance art has added to them so many implications, transmitted to the *and colouring*
aesthetic ideas of the following period, that they have become autonomous,
universal methods of visualization, each of which excludes the other; each of
them is able to express the whole range of visible phenomena through its
medium. A reconciliation between these two conflicting elements could not be
brought about merely by fusing them. Sebastiano del Piombo's solution, which
we mentioned above, was an attempt which may be explained as due to
exceptional personal circumstances. The recipe attributed to the Carracci, that

the perfect work of art may be achieved by the mixing together of hetero-
geneous talents, would be a contradiction if it did not formally circumscribe
a far more complicated state of affairs, in the same way as this is true of the
slogan: " Titian's colouring and Michelangelo's drawing " as applied to Tintoretto's art.   It would perhaps be more correct to say that each of the two
component parts of the formula in the original sense had to be mastered and
interpreted afresh, before the new unity could come to life which seems so
organic in Tintoretto's style.   For, however great the possibility of false judge-
ments as to details of his works, the general Tintorettesque element, the peculiar
fundamental tone, which determines the special feature of his art, should be
unmistakably accessible to intuitive comprehension.

About 1560, after being winnowed by means of numerous experiments,
this style achieved its definitive form of expression.   In the 1937 Mostra there
was perhaps no picture which revealed to such an extent the strength of acquired
The Last Supper
in San Trovaso
Fig. 88
confidence as the Last Supper from San Trovaso, the new and remarkable
conception of which was praised by the old Ridolfi.   That this subject was
depicted by Tintoretto both before and afterwards more frequently than any
other made it all the more suitable for trying out Tintoretto's new attitude to
Fig. 20
form and colour.   The oldest version is that in San Marcuola, in which the
adherence to the older Venetian schemes of composition and the subservience to
the conception of colouring dominated by Titian are still noticeable.   But
this does not mean that personal features characteristic of Tintoretto are lacking.
The two women at the sides, whose humble figures are so unconstrainedly filled
with the allegorical conception of Faith and Charity, are not only typical of
that group of characteristics which can be deduced from his early works and
which constitute his early style, but they are also real offspring of Tintoretto's
mind, the sisters of the innumerable women who will people his compositions
down to the glorious epic of San Rocco.   But the unmistakably Tintorettesque
element has not yet attained the full density which it achieves in the Last Supper
in San Trovaso; the personal element is still too deeply immersed in school
influences.

Composition
In the San Trovaso picture the central arrangement, fruit of centuries of
development, is abandoned and replaced by an oblique composition the germs of
which are already to be found in Titian.   But the latter, in his Pesaro Madonna
and similar pictures, did not deliberately dissolve the fundamental cohesion of
the planes, whereas in Tintoretto's painting an entirely new conception of space
is created.   In the San Marcuola picture, too, projection into depth was not
entirely lacking.   The pattern of the pavement leads the eye towards the
background—like other aids to vision which are characteristic of a whole group
of pictures from his early period—and in the same way we find a striving to
obtain greater depth of setting, such as the older Venetian painters, and in
exceptional cases Titian himself, sought to achieve.   In the San Trovaso pictures
intention and result are both different.   In the older version in San Marcuola
rational methods are employed, the setting of the figure composition, pressed

into the plane, being deepened to a measurable extent, while behind this it is shut off completely. In the Last Supper in San Trovaso, on the other hand, the foreground is brought into relation with endless depth without obvious means of compulsion, by means of the obliquely placed staircase on the left, immersed in semi-darkness and terminating mysteriously, and the hall with its open arcades on the right, the influx of light from which inundates two accessory figures. Foreground and background are one, an excerpt from infinity, but limited by the numerous parallel lines leading upwards towards the right; the right edge of the table set off by the overturned chair, the row of Apostles to the left, and in between—the spiritual axis of the picture—Jesus and Judas, and at the side the stairs and the still life; while those running from left to right intersect them with equal vigour; the cohesion with the plane is incomparably more vigorous than in San Marcuola; in the latter two tendencies were combined to form a compromise, in San Trovaso they are fused to a complete unity.

It was not only in the composition of the San Trovaso picture that Tintoretto struck his own note; in the colouring, too, he followed other laws than those which he obeyed during the tentative years filled with memories of Titian. In this respect the Last Supper in San Marcuola with its heavy local colouring goes back further than Titian—or rather is derived from other contemporary Venetian painters as well as Titian—, but other pictures from about the same period—especially the first Miracle of St. Mark painted in 1548 and the almost contemporary Miracle of St. Agnes in Madonna dell'Orto—stand under the sign of his revelation of colour as the determining factor in pictorial effect. In San Trovaso this wealth of colour is dispensed with, the luxurious splendour is toned down; Tintoretto's art is none the poorer, for in his maturity he knew how to achieve tender effects and delicate colour, but it is as if its impetus were broken, its frankness subdued rather than its brightness. His tendency to monochrome has been emphasized far too much as a determining factor in Tintoretto's coloristic development; the bad state of preservation and the unfortunate positions of many important pictures have led to it being overlooked that a progressive subduing of colour and an increase of variety are two results of the same aim—to change the significance of colour. It is not only that, together with the pictures of the "green style", which all agree in attributing to the special conditions under which the San Rocco pictures were produced, others of radiant colouring were created, but in addition to this, in one and the same picture the method of using one or the other colour-principle varies, so that colour emphasizes and deepens colourlessness, and vice versa. That is to say, the colouring, which before aimed at being beautiful and charming, is deprived of its absolute value and dedicated to the service of expression and of the composition. Many of the late pictures have a gayer variety of colour than any of the earlier works, but their variety does not spring from the wish to create an equivalent of the infinite wealth of nature, the planes and patches of colour being clearly conceived, combining with one

Colouring

Fig. 20

Figs. 21, 27

Fig. 88

another like the elements of a mosaic, in order to express a wellbalanced vision. The bold manner in which colourlessness and variety of colour are mastered achieves its full maturity—and this is a symbol of the spiritual schism in which Tintoretto's artistic development culminated—only during the master's late period. But even at the time of the Last Supper in San Trovaso there are signs that the colouring, without at first becoming materially different, is undergoing an ideological change. In the course of thorough and ingenious studies Erich von der Bercken has traced the progress of the general toning down of Tintoretto's colours in every sphere of his art. This decline of warmth was not a physiological, but a psychological process. What makes Titian's colouring so enchanting, even when it occasionally indulges in dissonances, is its intrinsic magnificence, the independence with which it—and it alone—gives form and life to the inexhaustible worlds of earthly and spiritual creations. Tintoretto's colouring is deposed from this proud throne; it is the servant of composition and expression, and, instead of being a value in itself, is a means towards an end, despite the shreds of purely sensual beauty which, like a queen in exile, it carries with it, subordinated to another optic principle, namely light. Already in the Last Supper this factor has achieved its dominant position; the way in which the streaming light—which has no visible source—lifts the figures of the Saviour and his Disciples out of the darkness and spreads itself until it is checked by the dark corners at the top of the picture, is a paraphrase of the mystery which is taking place at the brightly lit table; even at this early stage the colouring plays no independent part. Later Tintoretto's lighting becomes more conscious of its possibilities and achieves the glorious freedom and wealth of expression which Titian's colour possessed.

Disintegration of form

Fig. 88

But we must first return to the example of the Last Supper in San Trovaso and note that a diminution of the form values runs parallel with the toning down of the colouring. It has been rightly said that this Last Supper is the most superficial of Tintoretto's great renderings of the theme, and gives to the single figures too much independence, if we measure them by the standard of the versions in San Polo, San Rocco and San Giorgio. In this respect, too, the picture represents a transition, the opening of a new era and the close of an old. The poses are too deliberate and too tense, their variety seems intentional, and the execution of the figures with their wealth of movement too obtrusive. It is true that they are brought into relationship with one another— the way in which several of the figures press towards the centre in the shape of a wedge, while others, to heighten the tension, bend outwards, is a presage of the future—but the weightiness of the single figures is a relic of the past. In the Miracle of St. Mark painted in 1548 Venice had beheld with wonder for the first time a painting in which every single figure was separately formed as in Florentine painting and the whole construction was composed of a number of elements, for the plasticity of which there was so to speak documentary evidence. Miracles of foreshortening, of statics and dynamics and of plastic vitality appeared before the eyes of those who had been directly or indirectly

PRESENTATION IN THE TEMPLE.
About 1540 (?). Venice, Santa Maria del Carmine.

CHRIST WITH SAINTS MARK AND GALLUS.
About 1540 (?). Venice, San Gallo.

PLATE III

CHRIST ON THE SEA OF GALILEE. Washington, National Gallery of Art, Kress Collection

touched by Michelangelo's magic wand. But we feel that there was rather too much wondering at the wonders. The mighty forms move clumsily like young giants, make the composition swell and boom forth its pathos; in the pictures painted in the 1550's—the Evangelists in Santa Maria Zobenigo, the Paradise pictures from the Trinità in the Accademia, the Presentation of the Virgin in Madonna dell'Orto or the Legend of St. Roch we see the preparation of this Pool of Bethesda in the church of San Rocco—we see Tintoretto's delight in form leading to solutions akin to those of Central Italian manneristic painting. Something of this excessive emphasis laid on the single figures is still perceptible in the Last Supper in San Trovaso, but also definite attempts to overcome it. The way in which the figures are related with one another and withdrawn into themselves, in which the picture is so filled with rhythmic life that each separate figure, however ostentatious its gestures, yet forfeits its right to separate existence, all that is already the perfected style of Tintoretto. And at the same time it is the full expression of a new era, which humbly dedicated its formal virtuosity to the service of the new spirituality. The renunciation of Renaissance modes of thought in the Last Supper produced a deep impression on that advocate by vocation of the Renaissance, Jakob Burckhardt; the Last Supper in San Trovaso is the one which his "Cicerone" decries as "degraded to a common banquet." It was not so much—as Thode assumed when defending the picture—the over-emphasis on all kinds of realistic accessories—the scanty furniture, mean clothing, food, crockery—which offended the taste of the classicists, as the upsetting of an arrangement sanctified by tradition and the depreciation of the individual in the interests of a new system. Burckhardt was not so sensitive as to be upset by an overturned chair; but he was consequential enough not to let himself be led by the dramatic vigour and psychological refinements to forget that here everything was rejected which according to his conception constituted art. Burckhardt refused to recognize Tintoretto not because of any specific aesthetic considerations, but because he was bound to reject the whole essence of his art.

The Last Supper in San Trovaso, from which we have tried to deduce the elements of this art, thus stands as a prominent landmark on the ridge separating two periods; it is the introduction to the middle period of Tintoretto's activity, no longer encumbered with the learning acquired at school, which, while tentatively seeking its path like the early period, has not yet attained the self-assurance which characterizes Tintoretto's style in his old age, when he masters the forms of expression of the period and without thought for anything else aims only at artistic fulfilment. Tintoretto's middle period—like that of any other artist—is more objective, and because it lacks both the excessive temperamentality of his youth and the lonely self-seeking of his old age, it is the clearest reflection of the style to which he aspired. Inserted between two magnificent anarchies, it is an expression of orthodoxy. The works of the middle period give the most concise view of the master's formal theories.

Figs. 51, 52,
28-31, 98-100,
50, 72

Fig. 88

Marco Boschini, to whom we owe our knowledge of how Titian worked, also assembled from among the statements of pupils what was known about Tintoretto's procedure. When he had to paint a work for public display he first studied the general conditions of lighting and space on the spot. Then he prepared with his own hands little wax figures, which he assembled in their proper places in the composition under artificial lighting on a little stage constructed by himself. When he had thus finished the distribution of the figures, he sketched the whole picture in chiaroscuro, always endeavouring to harmonize the whole mass to one tone. When he subsequently tested on the spot a large canvas prepared in this way, it was often necessary to move, not only one figure, but many others round about it.

That Tintoretto's interest in the single figures was considered a novelty, and also was a novelty, we know already. He experimented with increasing zeal the feeling for life, which means the acknowledgement and reproduction of organic growth, and laboured incessantly to penetrate the secret of this living relationship. Drawings after works of sculpture were a means to this end, and the derivation of many of his single figures from such models can be detected; the companion of Arsinoë in the Dresden picture is derived from the same sculpture—but turned in a different direction—as the Susanna in Vienna. But with such a procedure we must naturally not imagine that Tintoretto relied only on auxiliary models prepared by himself or supplied to him by sculptors, for instance Roccatagliata; these were in any case for the most part much more primitive resources. Between the plastic model and the execution of the picture, there must often have come studies from the living nude; between the above-mentioned relief by Gianbologna and the Christ in the Vienna Flagellation, there comes a study from life which has been preserved in the Uffizi. In the plastic masterpieces from which he made his drawings, the concentration on three-dimensionality provided him with the greatest stimulus; and in the living nudes which he studied afterwards he found the same energy in a looser form. There must have been thousands of studies from life by Tintoretto; in the will of his son Domenico, who inherited the contents of his father's workshop, hundreds of them are disposed of, and the eighteenth-century writers were astonished at the enormous mass of material still in circulation in their time. What has been preserved of them and sifted, thanks to Hadeln's critical care, consists of studies from the nude and draped figures, the former being in part studies for figures which appeared draped in the finished pictures. It was Tintoretto's custom to prepare the draped female figures which appear in his pictures by means of studies from nude male models. We find similar material in the case of Raphael and other Central Italian artists; but while they studied the nude to clarify their ideas of plastic form, for Tintoretto the essential was not the body in itself, but the body in movement; not muscles but their function.

Among the single figures in Tintoretto's pictures, therefore, we do not find the man of muscles such as is prominent in other productions of manneristic

Fig. 64
Coloured plate

Fig. 243

Fig. 173

art; nor do we find the predilection for swollen muscles and obtrusive postures; Tintoretto's figures are slender and elongated, movable in all their limbs and moving in all directions. Their striking vitality they owe to the convincing realism with which they use their limbs. Especially at the beginning their proportions are long, their movements expressive, their gestures extremely articulated; as he becomes more and more master of his art, Tintoretto abandons these aids, his figures become more ordinary and their gestures, as has been rightly observed, wander from the tips of their fingers to their wrists and from there to their arms. His experience renders it possible for him to make his figures behave and move naturally—whether they are draped or nude, passionately agitated or tranquil. These postures and movements, however, have no pretensions to gymnastic precision; they do not, so to speak, take place on a firm stage, but on the rolling deck of a ship in rough sea.

However carefully he studied them, Tintoretto's single figures were never more than component parts of the whole they went to form; if the position of one of them had to be changed, then, as we read above, all the others round it were affected. The settling of these relationships was likewise a part of the *Conception of space* preparation of the picture. The process of building up the composition with little model figures on a miniature stage was also followed by other artists; but none of them shows the effort to balance plane and depth so consequentially accomplished as does Tintoretto. The logical construction of space was in accordance with the rational element in his character typical of the time, the annulment of this construction corresponded to his own irrational personal nature. Just as traces of his striving after plastic individuality are found only exceptionally in an unaltered form in his finished pictures, so too his aids to the achievement of spatial depth are rarely perceptible. In his youthful works Tintoretto delighted in such architectonic constructions; he placed his compositions in complicated halls or filled his backgrounds with imaginary architecture in faultless perspective, such as Bonifazio and Paris Bordone loved. He too was seized by that craze for rational mastery of space, of which Vasari wrote to Varchi just at the time in question—in 1547—that "perspective views of buildings, landscapes, mountains and rivers cause such pleasure that no cobbler's house is without its German landscapes." But all this miniature architecture soon disappeared; after the Miracle of St. Mark *Fig. 21* painted in 1548 the bodies in greatly heightened proportions fill up the space by themselves. In connection with this there appears a more intensive spatial construction for the eye—as in the Munich Venus, Vulcan and Cupid and in *Fig. 56* related pictures down to the Vienna Susanna—but it was not until the beginning of the 1560's that the problem again became important for Tintoretto. The Invention of the Cross with its model architecture in the background is already a return to the ideas of earlier pictures, and in the Marriage at Cana of 1561 *Fig. 116* in Santa Maria della Salute the setting is completely and carefully constructed; the help given by the table running into depth, the timbered ceiling, the enclosing walls, in leading the eye to the point of vision placed far to the left, immediately above the head of Christ, cannot be denied, although the edges of the table, overhung by the guests, the trend towards depth of the walls, broken by numerous embrasures, the movement of the ceiling beams owing to the swaying decorative pennants, are weakened. Perhaps the woman standing in the centre with her Netherlandish kerchief and the genre figures in the background are traces of a Northern—perhaps graphical—source, which had incited Tintoretto to a rational conquest of space. In any case the stimulus persisted; *Figs. 112, 113* in the pictures narrating the story of the Body of St. Mark at the Brera and in Venice (1562), the setting—whether in the open or indoors—is constructed as a transparent stage, with projection into depth and obstacles, as if aiming *Folding plate* at an ideal solution. In the large Crucifixion in San Rocco (1565) this overemphasis is toned down, the spatial construction becomes a means of expression, a thing taken for granted and not an aim of the composition. "In other words, this enormous canvas is a great sea of air and light, at the bottom of which the scene takes place. Without the atmosphere and the correct distribution of light it would, despite the crowd and the emotion, seem as dead and arid as the bottom of a dried-up sea" (Berenson).

Just as the single figure loses its individual value, so space is reduced to *Figs. 135, 136* a mere receptacle of atmosphere. In the two big pictures of St. Roch in the church of San Rocco this depreciation of space is veiled in a romantic twilight, which also permeates the sinister precincts of Limbo in the San Cassiano picture *Figs. 143, 144* of 1568; in the companion picture, the Crucifixion, the adjustment of planes and depth is still somewhat violent—the one by means of the seated figure of the Virgin and the undulating line of the warriors' heads, the other by means *Fig. 140* of the oblique placing of the crosses. In the Last Supper in San Polo, which may have been painted about the same time, we find for the first time the fusion, peculiar to Tintoretto, of spatial and non-spatial elements which dominated the whole of his late period. Clearly marked finiteness does not lose itself in endlessness, but in infinity; spatial depth, from the premiss of natural existence, becomes the image of supernatural vitality.

The transformation of the single figure ran parallel with that of space. The former loses its value, which the followers of Michelangelo's talent had so humbly adored, nowhere more completely than in works of mature Baroque art, where it degenerates into nothing more than a part of the whole; with Tintoretto it still retains this much significance, that as silhouette, as conveyor of movement, as element of pictorial rhythm, it is still conceived as clearly present. It is not fused with the composition, but built into it. This explains the infinite care Tintoretto took with his preliminary work and the infinite variety of his solutions.

Linear composition In the third chapter of their book Bercken and Mayer have systematically classified and examined the various devices of Tintoretto's linear composition; they have shown what frequent use he made of parallels, planimetric forms, movement and counter-movement. He attached great value to silhouettes; whether they stand out darkly against a bright sky, so that the latter is covered

with a filigree network—Last Judgement in Madonna dell'Orto, Crucifixion *Figs. 91, 93 a,*
in San Cassiano, Deposition in Caën, Rescue of the Slave in the Accademia— *144-145, 142,*
or whether they are so embedded in a thick mass of figures that they bind the *111*
composition together like a chain—Last Supper in San Trovaso and San Polo,
Invention of the Cross in Santa Maria Mater Domini, the Crucifixions from *Figs. 88, 140,*
San Severo and in San Rocco and, opposite the latter, the Bearing of the Cross *87, 117, folding*
and Christ before Pilate—the figures always seem to form impressive and *plate, 124, 125*
mysterious hieroglyphics and it is natural that we should be reminded by such
creations of German graphics. Nevertheless they constitute a natural stage in
the course of Tintoretto's development, which gradually reduces the single
figures and spatial depth to a calligraphic play of lines and, in the mature
style of the master's old age, as we shall presently see, subordinates all the
elements to a kind of musical rhythm.

The process of toning down the colouring moves in the same direction. *Toning down*
The colour becomes more and more independant of the object depicted and *of colouring*
therefore more mobile, more adaptable to the varying needs of expression; the
versatility of Tintoretto's colouring in this middle period is astounding and
confusing. The sonorous magnificence of colour in the Presentation of the
Virgin, the exuberance—perhaps inspired by Pordenone's example—of the Pool *Figs. 72, 117,*
of Bethesda in San Rocco, the harshness, comparable to Gothic pictorial effects, *144, 118, 124,*
in the Crucifixion in the Accademia and the solemn gloom of the other *125*
Crucifixion in San Cassiano, the heavy momentum of the Pietà in the Accademia
and the subdued solemnity of the scenes from the Passion in the Sala del-
l'Albergo of the Scuola di San Rocco—all these belong to the same decade. Their
remarkable variety has this common factor, that nowhere is colour used for the
sake of its own beauty or in order to provide transitions rich in nuances from
one portion of the picture to the other; on the contrary the patches of colour
lie close together but clearly distinguished, the aim being to give, not a close-up
view of reality, but a vision from a distance, thus preparing the way for the
still more consequential coloured mosaic effects of the late style. In this transformation of colour, the increasing importance attached to light plays a decisive
part. The lighting is irrational, in the interiors neither the daylight streaming
in from outside—Marriage at Cana—nor an artificial source of light is the *Fig. 116*
deciding factor, and when the scene is out of doors—as in the three Crucifixions of this decade—every attempt at naturalism of atmosphere is avoided.
Even when lighting effects are as important as they are in the two pictures
narrating the story of the Body of St. Mark—the Brera picture, in which the *Figs. 112, 113*
reflection of the torches flickers along the walls of the vault and the harshly-
lighted raised tombstone forms the point of vision at the end of a dark tunnel,
or in the picture in Venice with the smouldering atmosphere of an incipient
thunderstorm—even in these pictures the observation of reality is dedicated to
the achievement of spiritual effect. The figures carry their light in themselves
and radiate it—glowing with health like the Vienna Susanna, whose radiancy
illuminates the whole garden, or glimmering like ghosts, as, for example, the

Angels in the Limbo or in the Death of St. Roch. In his bold handling of his
unlimited possibilities Tintoretto anticipates many of Rembrandt's achievements.
Like Rembrandt, the Venetian master devises a whole world out of the inwardly
related categories of light and movement.

*Attitude
to reality*

        This brings us to the question of Tintoretto's attitude to reality. Devotees
of classicism like Jakob Burckhardt never grow weary of stigmatizing his
naturalism; even a writer so imbued with the genius of Tintoretto as Ruskin is
sometimes startled by the earthliness of many of his pictures. The Last Supper
Figs. 88, 112,
129, 135, 136
in San Trovaso has already provided us with an example of this; Tintoretto's
realistic daring horrified some and won the admiration of others, as did many
similar details such as the foreshortened corpse in the Finding of St. Mark's
Body, the warriors and servants in the San Rocco Crucifixion, the sick and the
prisoners who transform the two scenes from the life of the Saint who healed
the plague into hospital and prison art. The aim of this passion for natural
details was the creation of a feeling of life; but whereas this discovery of
reality determines the whole essence of the picture in the works of earlier and
later masters of this tendency—Konrad Witz and Masaccio, Caravaggio or
Ribera—with Tintoretto it serves merely to emphasize the unreal elements.
It is the striking impressiveness of beautifully painted details, of which we
have tried to give an idea by including many detail photographs among our
illustrations, that creates the setting for the spiritual event which is being
depicted; the photographic fidelity in the rendering of furniture, the virtuoso's
trick of foreshortened bodies serve to intensify the supernatural significance of
the subject. Scenes from the Passion or from the legends of Saints endeavour
to achieve their higher function not by means of carefully balanced composition,
idealistic exaltation of the human types or meditative impregnation of natural
objects, but by a devotion to the deepest significance of the subject and its
deliberate spiritualization. Tintoretto is one of those great Christian painters
to whom, out of the depths of their temperaments and the strength of their
religious beliefs, it was granted to interpret and transform in accordance with
the needs of their own time the traditional sacred subjects. What in the hands
of the older Renaissance artists had become a narration of historical events
becomes with Tintoretto the representation of an event which takes place in the
realm of the spirit. Scholars, both in the past and in more recent times, have
frequently used the long series of Last Suppers to show how the ephemerality of
the historical happening is transmuted more and more clearly into the time-
lessness of the religious mystery, how the story of the Passion, as narrated in
the Gospels, is considered more and more exclusively the mystery of the
Eucharist. This transmutation coincides with the religious revival during the
second half of the sixteenth century. Tintoretto's art is the expression of a new
spirit of the age, not only because the religious subject-matter is transformed in
accordance with direct experience, but also because the world of mythology,
which the philosophy of the Renaissance had to a certain extent co-ordinated
with Christian thought, now loses its element of self-understood existence.

When Titian painted a mythological subject, he instilled into it the atmosphere in which it had originally been created; for Tintoretto such subjects were a matter of knowledge, suitable for decorative purposes, a means of instruction which the spirit of the Reformation, still impregnated with humanism, had not yet discarded, but no longer a living source of inspiration. For this reason Titian's mythological pictures, however much they may be filled with a kind of inner relationship, are often obscure to the point of being unrecognizable, whereas his religious pictures as a rule offer no riddles of interpretation. With Tintoretto, on the other hand, mythological subjects, because they are conceived only from the intellectual standpoint, are clearly narrated, whereas his religious world is full of the obscurity of things actually experienced.

But experience and knowledge are subordinated to the same formal law; they are inserted into the linear and chromatic rhythm of the pictures, and logically utilized as formal elements quite independently of their inner relationships. The subjects, permeated with deep spiritual feeling, are transformed, in so far as they are artistically moulded, into component parts of a decoration, the increasing grace and splendour of which represent a prominent feature in Tintoretto's art. That their deep earnestness does not prevent their being used as material for the free play of artistic formation is perhaps the decisive factor in the understanding of Tintoretto's individuality. Once again we perceive the contrast between Titian's unity, resting upon itself, and Tintoretto's divided nature. As a result of a harmonization of content and form, both components are unilaterally enhanced; the subordination to the laws of art becomes more implicit and the need for spiritual expression more imperative. Tintoretto's art is deeply serious and at the same time boundlessly playful; it had its share—in conformity with its chronological position—in the formation of mannerism and early Baroque. Such stylistic denominations are abstractions from the currents which flowed through the period in many directions; they denote principles which are not strictly limited and do not exist side-by-side to the exclusion of one another, but which enter into an innumerable variety of associations with individual creators and creations. Tintoretto was a mannerist and a Baroque artist. In the mature phase of his art during the last years of his life this double quality will appear still more clearly.

II

TINTORETTO'S LIFE AND TRAINING

Literary sources

VERY LITTLE has been handed down to us concerning Tintoretto's life and professional career, although two biographies appeared during his lifetime; one added by Vasari to the second edition of his great work on Italian painters (1567), the other by Raffaele Borghini in his "Discorsi" on the theory of art (1584). While these two Florentine writers had to rely on material collected during occasional visits to Venice or communicated to them by correspondents residing in that city, Carlo Ridolfi, the first who after Tintoretto's death undertook to write a description of his whole life, was able to draw on the whole of Venetian tradition. That he was particularly pleased with the result of his efforts may be deduced from the fact that Ridolfi published his Vita of Tintoretto separately in 1642 as a specimen of his projected collection of biographies of Venetian artists, and included it without any substantial alteration in the main work which appeared six years later. Later on in the Baroque period, that Venetian author and local patriot Marco Boschini made further contributions to our knowledge of Tintoretto in his curious "Carta del navigare pittoresco" (1660) and in his more systematic "Minere della pittura veneziana" (1664). Although Boschini wrote long after Tintoretto's death, his books are none the less important, because he was in contact with the atelier which had continued working after the master's death, and of all the older art historians had the most thorough understanding of the peculiarities of Venetian painting.

Dates

Despite this abundance of literary sources, supplemented by all kinds of documents, the resulting information is meagre enough; we can deduce from it hardly more than the bare outlines of Tintoretto's life. He was born in the autumn of 1518—not, as was formerly supposed, in 1512—his father being the dyer Battista Robusti; from his father's profession—"tintore"—Jacopo received the nickname of Tintoretto. He died on May 31st, 1594. Between these dates he led a simple bourgeois existence, the most important dates in which are the following: On May 22nd, 1539, Tintoretto, who was then living in the parish of San Cassiano, describes himself in a document as "master", that is to say as an independent craftsman. Later he moved to the other side of the Grand Canal to the parish of San Marciliano. In 1550 he married Faustina dei Vescovi, who bore him several children; of these, Marietta, born about 1552, Domenico, born before 1560, and Marco, followed their father's profession; a daughter named Ottavia married the painter Sebastiano Casser, while the others entered convents. Tintoretto must have lived in prosperous conditions, for from the middle of the century on he was increasingly occupied with official commissions, executing numerous works for the Ducal Palace, for other public buildings and for San Marco, but above all for the Brotherhoods—especially for the "Schools" of San Rocco and San Marco—which gave him constant and extensive orders, while in addition to this he also painted for other churches and for private customers. In 1574 he purchased through his father-in-law the house near the Madonna dell'Orto, which after his death passed to his son Domenico and then to the latter's heir and business successor, his brother-in-law Casser. Nevertheless Tintoretto never became a wealthy man. His efforts to have the fees for his works paid to him in the form of regular annuities show that, like Titian, he considered a fixed income a better economic basis than the fluctuating receipts from occasional commissions. As payment for his large picture glorifying the Battle of Lepanto in the Ducal Palace, he asked in 1571 that he should be given the reversion of a brokership in the Fondaco dei Tedeschi, which would bring him in a hundred ducats a year, and in 1577 he concluded an agreement with the Scuola di San Rocco, by virtue of which he was to receive the same sum every year in settlement of his continuous artistic activity on behalf of the school. From the records of payments which have been preserved we know that he actually received these sums, whereas his income from the state remained on paper only, for in 1600 his widow Faustina complained to the Signoria that he had not received a single payment, and in view of the poor circumstances in which her husband had left her and her children, she asked for a monthly subsidy of twelve ducats.

One or two anecdotes related by his biographers depict Tintoretto as a bad manager where money matters were concerned; this attribute, so typical of artists, was augmented by his fanatical obsession about obtaining orders by any means. The story is related in various forms, that in order to be able to execute a work that interested him, he was prepared to do it at cost price or even for less. According to Vasari, he obtained in this way a very large part of the orders for paintings given in Venice during his time. The reason which induced Tintoretto to undercut his competitors in this way cannot—at all events in the majority of cases—have been the desire for money; it was more probably a craving to create, which formed the sometimes not very agreeable reverse side of his otherwise admirable productivity. When a commission for a work of art was in the balance, this great and earnest master did not shrink from petty business devices. When the Crociferi hesitated to entrust him with the painting of the picture for their high altar, because they would have preferred a work by Paolo Veronese, Tintoretto undertook to paint it in the style of that master, and actually did it; the marked adaptability shown in his early works may have been due to similar motives. He repeatedly obtained orders by furtive means. There is a circumstantial story of how in 1564, in the competition for a ceiling-painting in the Sala dell'Albergo

Anecdotes

Fig. 122

at the Scuola di San Rocco, he did not submit a design like the other competitors, but, against the conditions laid down, introduced a finished picture into
the hall, thus placing the members of the Scuola face to face with a *fait
accompli.* In a similar manner in 1571 he outwitted all the competitors for
the state competition for the official picture commemorating the victory of
Lepanto, by making a present of the finished picture to the Signoria, though
this did not prevent him from sending in a bill afterwards. Naturally we must
realize that such breaches of bourgeois decorum and professional etiquette had
their justification in the right of the artist to employ every means in the interest
of higher achievement, but it cannot be doubted that such lapses must have
irritated other painters and made Tintoretto unpopular perhaps in other circles
as well. When it was proposed to defray the cost of the ceiling-paintings in
the Sala dell'Albergo by means of a subscription to be levied on all the members,
a certain Messer Zammaria de'Zigninoni promised to contribute fifteen ducats
on the express condition that the work should be entrusted to another painter,
not to Tintoretto; and in fact he refused to pay anything when the latter's
picture was accepted. We do not know whether Zammaria was a pedantic
opponent of Tintoretto's art or merely a respectable burgher who disliked the
business methods of the impulsive artist. Many other members of the Confraternity also voted against the acceptance of Tintoretto's present. The behaviour
of the recipients in the case of the other picture which Tintoretto forced upon
his customers, the Battle of Lepanto, is perhaps even more significant. When
it was destroyed in the disastrous fire of 1577 at the Ducal Palace, the painting
of a substitute for it was not entrusted to Tintoretto, who in the meantime had
painted numerous other works for the Palace, but to the far more insignificant
Andrea Vicentino, who nevertheless received a considerably higher fee than
was paid for the original.

    Tintoretto's unpopularity among his colleagues is almost the only note-
worthy feature which we can deduce from the biographical sources; the other
anecdotes told about him—one or two rather feeble witticisms and a few
amusing stories about his private life—are more important for the general
atmosphere they convey than for their content. They show us a milieu and

Family life

a man notably different to Titian and his world. The pronounced family
feeling and also a certain similarity in the composition of the family are the
only things they had in common; Tintoretto was particularly attached to his
daughter, who was also bound to him by her work as a painter, and in his son
Domenico he found a useful collaborator and follower. In his will, Tintoretto left to Domenico, who had long been his right hand, the conduct
of the atelier after his death; the other son, who also painted in the atelier,
seems—as was also the case with Titian's Pomponio—not to have satisfied
his father. That was all that Titian and Tintoretto had in common. Tintoretto's professional and Venetian career was exactly like his bourgeois
private life. Except for a chance meeting with the famous visitor of 1574,
King Henri III of France, Tintoretto had no contact with the great ones of

this earth, he never tried to obtain court offices or titles, had no friendships with famous men of letters and hardly ever left his native city. There is historical evidence of only one journey made by him, when he went to Mantua in 1580 to deliver and arrange his series of scenes from the history of the Gonzagas; it is in keeping with the general picture of him that Tintoretto was unwilling to undertake this journey unless his wife could go with him. There was something humdrum about Tintoretto's existence, in contrast to Titian, about whom there hangs a certain glamour—on account of his art, it is true, but also on account of other things outside his art. The personality of Tintoretto is obliterated by his paintings; we can attribute to it hardly any characteristics which are not derived solely from his art.

Figs. 220-224

But the material available is not even sufficient to enable us to reconstruct his artistic development; how he arrived at the manner which we tried to outline in the first chapter as the peculiar Tintoretto style is not explained by any of his older biographers. Only on one point are they all agreed: that the boy, when he first began to show signs of his talent for painting, was sent as a pupil to Titian; but they state that the instruction lasted only a short time—probably only a few days—for the master was so jealous of his pupil's exceptional talent, that he at once sent him away. That does not sound so very incredible, at least in its essence; Titian had no liking for too independent pupils and it is very possible that the relationship of master and pupil very soon led to a break. Later on Titian never attempted to conceal his dislike for Tintoretto's art. What is incredible, however, is that which many writers want to deduce from the silence of the sources about Tintoretto having had any other teacher: namely, that after this first unsuccessful experience, Tintoretto had no other teacher but himself. That genius does not have to rely on the instruction of a second-rate teacher is obvious, but that is true of other artists besides Tintoretto; certainly, with the great receptiveness of his great talent he must have taken from Venetian painting as he found it all that he could use in his own art. But that in addition to this he should have been apprenticed to a teacher would have been in accordance with the custom of the time. Tintoretto himself, on whose statements the information given by his first biographer is based, evidently did not consider that he owed this master such a debt of gratitude as to make it incumbent upon him to preserve and hand down his name; for him Titian, who had rejected him, but whom he continued to look up to with admiration for the rest of his life, was his real teacher. After Titian's death he purchased several of the much-admired abbozzi which the master left behind.

Artistic beginnings

We cannot, however, rest altogether content with this version, inspired to a certain extent by the master himself. If Tintoretto already had his own workshop in 1539, when he was twenty-one years old, he must have matured very early and have created a considerable number of works in the decade preceding his first great public success in 1548 with the Rescue

Fig. 21

of the Slave. Of these, with the exception of a few isolated portraits, we
know only the Last Supper, dated 1547, in San Marcuola and possibly the
Figs. 20, 3 Contest between Apollo and Marsyas (formerly in the collection of Colonel
Bromley-Davenport), which in all probability is identical with a ceiling-
painting of this subject executed for Pietro Aretino in 1545. To these few
certainties we must, if we wish to reconstruct Tintoretto's youthful production,
add a number of pictures in which we believe we can detect analogies or
preliminary stages towards them; but the coursee of our search must inevitably
be uncertain, as we do not know what he started from, or what he knew
when he finished his schooling.

*Who was
Tintoretto's
teacher?*
Three artists have been suggested as most likely to have been Tintoretto's
teachers, and these were the heads of the three ateliers which, in addition to
Titian's, had an importance of their own: Bonifazio dei Pitati, Andrea
Schiavone and Paris Bordone. In favour of the first two we have vague
statements in the works of the old writers. Boschini mentions Bonifazio's
altar-piece in the Scuola of the tailors, and adds: round this room ran a frieze
with scenes from the legend of St. Barbara, painted in the early years of
Tintoretto's boyhood. Bonifazio's Conversazione, now in the Royal Palace,
is dated 1533; it seems not improbable that he may have employed the
prematurely mature fifteen-year-old Tintoretto to paint the decorations connected with it. While Tintoretto was still alive, he was credited with a
share in the painting of the sacristy in San Sebastiano, executed by Bonifazio
and his workshop. The feeling that Tintoretto must have studied under
Bonifazio has gained much support since Berenson first suggested it, and many
points of contact between the works of the two artists have been brought to
notice. But the objection has rightly been made that it is precisely in Tintoretto's youthful works that his influence of Bonifazio is least perceptible;
later, when Tintoretto continued the series of pictures executed by the older
master for the Camerlenghi, he obviously adapted himself—with that famous
talent of his for assuming another artist's style—to the art of Bonifazio, in one
Figs. 48, 49 case (the St. Jerome, St. Louis and St. Andrew) to such an extent that some critics
were tempted to assume a collaboration between the two masters. If Tinto-
retto had been Bonifazio's pupil, then the similarities ought to have been
still more prominent during the years of the greatest susceptibility to teaching
and of close contact in the studio; but the early pictures show nothing of the
striking relationship revealed by the works from the beginning of the 1550's.

*Andrea
Schiavone*
Tintoretto is said to have had an unusual admiration for Schiavone as a
master of colour; he gave it as his opinion, and Boschini quotes his words,
that every painter ought to have a picture by the Dalmatian artist in his
atelier, in order to learn from its beautiful colours. And Tintoretto did in fact
do this. According to Ridolfi, his enthusiasm was such that he collaborated with
Schiavone without asking for any payment, his aim being to master Schiavone's
technique. And in fact the older writers found that the works of the two artists
could easily be confused; the Presentation in the church of the Carmine, for

instance, was attributed by contemporary writers sometimes to one, sometimes to
the other. As for the cassone pictures, the confusion has lasted until our own
day; it is only a short time since some of the pictures of this kind have been
claimed for Tintoretto from among the great mass of those attributed to Schiavone.

As Schiavone must have been born earlier than tradition would have us
believe, the possibility that Tintoretto may have been his pupil cannot be
excluded; but on the other hand we can see no signs of his art having derived
anything from Schiavone's.   Here again there are only isolated similarities
and reminiscences, but Schiavone's art is far too elusive to make it possible to
affirm that certain mannerisms and colour features which we meet with in
Tintoretto must have been derived from him—and not direct from Schiavone's
inspirer Parmeggianino or other intermediaries. As with Bonifazio, here too
we seem to have nothing but separate, concrete points of contact. Tintoretto
was a diligent student, willing to learn from everybody; the sources relate
that he even had resource to masons in order to learn the best technique of
fresco, and he did not despise the hints which he could obtain from the crafts-
manship of the furniture-painters in Piazza San Marco. That he was in touch
with Schiavone is narrated in the same breath, with the remark that he
collaborated with him in frescoes.

Two categories of works must be taken into consideration when studying *Frescoes and*
the relationship between Schiavone and Tintoretto—cassoni and façade pain- *cassoni*
tings. Both belong to the class of works on which a Venetian painter of the
High Renaissance, at the beginning of his career, endeavoured to found his
professional existence; it seems plausible to assume that such works belong or
belonged among Tintoretto's early works.   Of the frescoes almost everything
has been lost, among them, unfortunately, a Belshazzar's Feast formerly at the
Arsenal, which was dated 1546 and for that reason would have been a valuable
document for us: others have at least been preserved for us in the engravings
of Zanetti, who made every effort to reproduce them faithfully in the eighteenth century. The frescoes on the Palazzo Grimani Gussoni, which are
generally cited as proof of the fact that the young Tintoretto studied Michelangelo, because they reproduce his Aurora and Crepuscolo in the Medici chapel,
we prefer to date from the 1550's, a period which, as we have seen, was a
kind of time-limit for his acquaintance with these figures; their powerful
postures agree in every way with pictures from this period (the Evangelists *Figs. 51, 52,*
in Santa Maria Zobenigo, the Last Judgement in Madonna dell'Orto, the *91, 72*
Pool of Bethesda in San Rocco). On the other hand the paintings on Palazzo
Soranzo dell'Angelo—insignificant fragments of which can still be seen on *Plate IV*
the building—may very well be assigned to the 1540's; the virtuoso's trick
of a frieze composed of hands and feet also points to an early period. It is not,
however, possible to say whether they bear a stronger resemblance to Schiavone
than to the works of other painters from whom Tintoretto drew inspiration—
for who has ever seen frescoes by Schiavone?

As to the cassoni, at first glance Schiavone's influence seems to be much greater. Hadeln recently attempted to distinguish his work from Tintoretto's, and undoubtedly the last word has still to be said on this question; it would be necessary to extend the investigation to a far greater number of works than Hadeln dealt with. But even the six Vienna panels, which he discussed

Figs. 32-46 thoroughly, perhaps reveal more than was believed hitherto; they do not constitute a homogeneous group, but the relationship is most noticeable between three pairs (175 and 157; 184 and 195; 184a and 203), and all they bear the stamp of Tintoretto. His influence is so strong as to make us overlook the differences; in addition to this, the fact that they were all destined for the same purpose produces a unifying effect, all the panels obeying the dictates of a " cassoni style " in the formation of which Schiavone, who until a short time ago was held to be the only representative of this craft, played an important part. Because they are cassoni, these pictures have long been neglected; if we compare details of them, which eliminate the uniform element, with other works by Tintoretto, we notice at once how essentially they differ from other works of this kind attributed with more justification to Schiavone. It should also be

Figs. 34, 35 noted that only the Revenge of Samson and the Prostration of Bathseba (?) have the dramatic intensity and the pictorial breadth of Tintoretto—at the time of the first Miracle of St. Mark; but that the other two pairs are permeated, to a varying extent, with Bonifaziesque and other old-fashioned or anomalous characteristics. In my opinion the explanation of this is, that such furniture paintings—like most other works of this kind—are workshop productions in the most literal sense, that is to say that a master like Tintoretto, even in his youth, did not execute such things personally, but had them carried out by his assistants under his artistic direction, he himself assuming the responsibility for them from a business point of view. The sketch for the left half of the Queen of Sheba in the Suermondt Museum at Aachen, which is closer to Tinto-

Figs. 40, 33 retto's own conception of form than the cassone picture itself and with its broad, almost crude brushwork very similar to the six Old Testament scenes in the Prado, is a very instructive document; all the elements are present, but in the finished picture they are combined in a different manner, and this freer arrangement was probably left to the workshop. That there were also Northerners in the latter, who were specialized in landscapes and still-life, is directly attested by the sources: among them Martin de Vos and Lambert Sustris are mentioned, the latter of whom left Venice in 1560. The workshop to which they belonged must therefore have been that of Tintoretto's early period; if I am not mistaken, the collaboration of these artists or of other assistants from Northern Europe can be detected in the routine superficiality of the Vienna cassoni—and also in the excessive amount of landscape in pictures such as the Paris Susanna, which is difficult to reconcile with Tintoretto's own personal predilections. Such methods of production naturally make it difficult to distinguish the pictures of this workshop from those of other ateliers such as Schiavone's or Bonifazio's, which were similarly constituted.

The links with these two artists resulting from the above-mentioned *Paris Bordone* similarities do not seem to me to represent a complete answer to the question of Tintoretto's schooling. I should be inclined to accept Hadeln's suggestion that Paris Bordone was his most likely teacher, if it were possible to recognize, instead of isolated similarities, a broader general connection with the works of his supposed pupil. Bordone had formerly been with Titian, and we may consider it possible, for psychological reasons also, that the young Tintoretto, after Titian had refused to instruct him, turned to the very man who had previously been rejected by Titian for similar reasons and in similar circumstances. More important still is that in this case the stylistic resemblance is not confined to isolated details, but can be traced in every element: in the types, the composition, the relationship between figures and landscape architecture, and in the colouring. A picture like Bordone's Last Supper in San Giovanni in Bragora, with its arrangement of the Apostles in two groups of five each on either side of the three chief figures in the centre of the scene and its flanking genre figures on the extreme edges, seems to me to constitute a direct forerunner of the Last Supper in San Marcuola; in the same way the *Fig. 20* Santa Conversazione in San Giobbe is likewise a preparation for Tintoretto. On the other hand pictures like the Saviour between Saints Gallus and Mark in San Gallo or the Calling of Peter in the Fogg Art Museum, Cambridge, Mass., *Plate 11* if they really are by Tintoretto, would be proofs that his style developed on the basis of Bordone's. The solution of the problem lies in establishing an organic derivation of this kind, far more than in the discovery of points of similarity between Tintoretto and various artists. A picture like Paris Bordone's Baptism of Christ in the Brera, even if it reveals no direct connection with Tintoretto, has perhaps more claim to be considered as a forerunner of Tintoretto's art than other pictures with which the varying productions of his early period are often compared.

The productions of this early period thus appear to us in a very uncertain *Early works* light. That they must have been considerable is warranted by the artist's great desire to create and by his early successes; the Scuola di San Marco would never have employed an artist without rank or reputation. But it is difficult to establish what they were, because there is no definite line of development linking the works with one another. The whole character of the first decade of Tintoretto's activity is that of an experiment; an experiment which had to be made, but whose provisional and ephemeral nature we ought to realize more than is generally done. Because one or two pictures of Tintorettesque style show traces of the art of Bonifazio, Schiavone or Bordone, it is assumed that Tintoretto was the pupil of these artists; and because this supposition already exists, the attribution to Tintoretto of the picture in question appears to be justified. We are not yet in a position to substitue certain means of recognition for these deceptive appearances, but we must beware of confusing constant supposition with certainty. Pictures like the Presentation in the church of the *Plate 11*

Carmine may be by Tintoretto, but only on the assumption that a reconstruction of his early training, based partly on this and other doubtful pictures, is correct.

Figs. 20, 21   We reach firmer ground in 1547—48 with the two dated masterpieces, the Last Supper in San Marcuola and the first Miracle of St. Mark. All the works preceding these—or supposed to precede them—are lacking in unity, variable, of uncertain intention; they contain, so to speak, so little of Tintoretto, and are strongly indebted to Venetian tradition before and at the time of Titian— a positive characteristic after so many negative criteria. They show a special predilection for frieze-like compositions consisting of elements all having the same value and concentrated in the foreground of the picture; the eye is led towards depth by obvious devices such as geometrical floor-patterns and carefully constructed architecture. These are principles which can be traced back to the Bellini and to Carpaccio and which continued in the new form given to them by Bonifazio. There is also a striking predominance of verticals in

Figs. 14, 15, 8 all of them. In the Rome and Amsterdam versions of the Woman taken in Adultery, in the Moses striking the Rock in Frankfurt, numerous perpendiculars are placed close together without being linked by any continuous movement. Similar tendencies are seen in the Miracle of the Loaves and Fishes in the

Fig. 9   Metropolitan Museum, which seems like a further development of the Frankfurt picture, the subjects also having a certain relationship; but in this case there is more decay than fusion, an exaggeration of single elements, enhanced by the delight in external exoticism—also a true Venetian characteristic. This superficial ornamentation in its turn enhances the doll-like nature of the slender, delicate and gesticulating little figures, whose movements are determined not by inner feeling but by external motives, as if strings were pulling them. The colour has an excessive warmth, with manneristic traits, and varies between emphasis on the pompous local colours and a tendency towards iridescent tones.

Fig. 11   The altar-piece of St. Ursula shows most cleary these characteristics of the still unformed style of Tintoretto; with its old-fashioned procession of stiff idol-like figures, receding in a solemn zigzag into height rather than into depth, there is hardly a single detail—with the exception of the swooping angel— which reminds us of the master's later style, and yet the restrained potential power gives the picture such an air of authenticity that it is impossible to have any doubts about it. It is a warning against any attempt to follow the mysterious growth of genius step by step.

It is thus difficult to determine the relationship of the above-discussed small-figure compositions to several large-figure works—the Woman taken in

Figs. 2, 4, 5, 3 Adultery in Dresden, the Visitation in Bologna, the Nativity of John the Baptist in San Zaccaria, all of which have points of contact with the Contest between Apollo and Marsyas, painted in 1545 and formerly in the Bromley-Davenport collection; they appear to have been painted more or less together, or at any rate at not very large intervals; the types show many resemblances, the treatment of space is the same, the colour moves at the same pace—and with the same jumps. But the altered relationship between the volume of the

PLATE IV

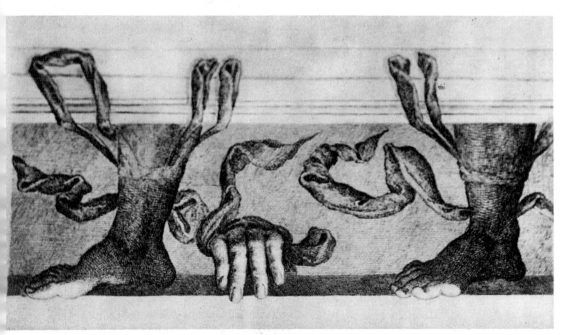

FRESCOES ON THE PALAZZO SORANZO IN VENICE. After etchings by G. M. Zanetti.

PLATE V

CEILING IN THE SALA DELLE QUATTRO PORTE. Venice, Ducal Palace.

figures and the pictorial plane creates new conditions. The single figure is
not only relative, but becomes more weighty; in this way it gains mass and
weight, intensity of movement and wealth of colouring.   All this gives
Tintoretto far greater possibilities of development than the limited dimensions
of his small-figure pictures permitted; the enlarged figures are filled with
strength of feeling, which they express with sustained gestures; silhouettes begin
to appear, the groups begin to be fused, movement begins to flow through the
frames of the figures. But when the real Tintoretto begins to appear, he is
no longer able to maintain unconditionally his rejection of Titian; the swelling
harmony of colour—for instance, the sonorous bluish red in the Nativity of
the Baptist—is derived from Titian's heroic period in the 1520's. The most
wonderful experience which Venice provided for a maturing artist could not be
suppressed by any obstinate resistance.

The restless and contradictory elements in Tintoretto's first period of
activity—the nature of which we can guess even though we cannot define it
exactly—seem to me to be most easily explained as a reaction against his love
for Titian. Repulsed by the teacher to whom he felt himself instinctively
drawn, he went as far as he could to the other extreme, to the painters who
had the custody of all Venetian tradition except that part of it which was
Titianesque, to the craftsmen from whom he tried to glean all the secrets of
their technique. He could utilize everything, but the imperative need to devote
himself to a revered model remained unsatisfied. The time was bound to come
when he would be unable to resist any longer the attraction of Titian, and this
crisis in his life seems to have been imminent about 1547.

In that year Tintoretto painted the Last Supper in San Marcuola,   *Fig. 20*
circumstantially authenticated by signature and date. Its companion piece,
the Washing of Feet now in the Escorial, is not dated and also differs from
it stylistically, which has led scholars to date it sometimes before and sometimes
after the Last Supper. Without going further into this question we may note
that in this dissimilar pair of pictures the two tendencies come to an end the
conflict between which dominated the restless early period. The Washing of
Feet belongs to the group of pictures of small calibre, the Last Supper to the
opposite group; in both the Bonifazio-Schiavone element may be discerned in
the types and colouring, but in both the Tintorettesque elements appear more
clearly than before. Several of the Apostles in the Washing of Feet bear his
mark unmistakably, but they are still isolated, not linked together, specimens
of his personal style rather than the mature fruits thereof. In the Last Supper
his realization of himself has progressed still further. When we compared it
with the version of the same subject in San Trovaso, we drew attention to   *Fig. 88*
its old-fashioned qualities; we must now emphasize more forcibly the emergence
of the essentiel Tintorettesque features. The way in which the compositional
scheme is kneaded together, in which a wave of vital movements traverses the
compact group of thirteen figures, while the two women enframing the compo-

sition at the sides combine everyday occupations with symbolical significance, all this is a presage of the later qualities which distinguish the master in his full maturity.

Emergence of
his own style
Fig. 21

1548

Nevertheless the sensation of the following year comes as a complete surprise. The Rescue of the Slave by St. Mark is not only new in its composition and treatment of the single figures, but still newer in its vital feeling and self-consciousness. Here the spectator is engulfed by the jubilant confidence of a great artist who has found himself. We ask ourselves whether it is really true, as is generally assumed, that Michelangelo helped him to find himself, whether it was actual contact with this mighty personality, perhaps in Rome, which brought about this profound transformation.

Both the enrichment of the plastic elements and the condensation of the composition have been attributed to inspiration from this quarter. In the powerful poses of the figures seated at the judge's feet on the right and in the woman leaning backwards on the left the pathos of Michelangelo is perceptible, and some writers have claimed that the sculptured figures on the portal of the garden in the background are a direct borrowing from the Medici tombs; the chief motif of the composition, the contrast between the slave lying on the ground and St. Mark swooping down to his rescue, is derived, according to Max Dvořák, from Michelangelo's Conversion of St. Paul, but this association seems to me to reveal the fundamental difference rather than any similarity. The magnificent figure composition in the Paolina extends and even creates space with its diagonals, whereas in the Miracle of St. Mark the gradation of the figures into depth, and above all the lane which the foreshortened nude figure of the slave opens up towards the back, is in no wise different from the foreground arrangement which Tintoretto, in conformity with Venetian tradition, used in order to limit his compositions. It is true that this shallow foreground has undergone transformation both as regards form and feeling, as compared with earlier pictures, but the background is only a foil for setting off the importance of the episode in the foreground. The plastic wealth of the single figures, too, is not an end in itself, but a premise; the materials constituting the picture are thereby enhanced and rendered more vigorous— the stage is filled with important actors, who act with pathos, but the declamatory element in this wonderful picture is fundamentally different from Michelangelo's pathos. The essential feature in it seems to me to be, as Thode so aptly expressed it, the creation of a monumental style for wall-paintings in Venetian art, whereas even the largest works of Titian were conceived and executed as panel-paintings.

Tintoretto
and Michel-
angelo

All this does not exclude the possibility that Tintoretto drew inspiration from Michelangelo, but it makes it doubtful whether the stimulus came to him as the result of direct contact. This susceptible artist, who was so willing to give himself whole-heartedly to an example or a model, would have been more deeply impressed by personal acquaintance with Michelangelo himself; he would not—or at all events not at first—have reacted to the merciless logic of the Paolina fresco with such an unchaining of all pictorial means of expression producing an effect of the greatest unity. A journey to Rome—especially just before this picture—would have left more definite traces; in this picture we cannot recognize with certainty even the study of actual sculptures such as is perceptible in his later drawings and pictures. Michelangelo cannot have encountered Tintoretto with all the irresistible force of his whole personality, but must have been transmitted to him gradually, and in conjunction with other elements.

That the Venetians were acquainted with the problems of Central Italian art is no new discovery. In 1539, the year in which Tintoretto first emerged as an independent painter, Francesco Salviati painted his Psyche cycle in Palazzo Grimani; in 1541 Giuseppe Salviati settled in Venice and held a successful performance in the presence of Vasari; in addition to this, graphic art transmitted knowledge of compositions, types and motives. Tintoretto eagerly absorbed all these factors from the manneristic art of Florence, but he did not become its slavish imitator; and he too absorbed what he could use only in the course of time. There is nothing to show that he fell in love with it at first sight and abandoned all his previous ideas. In Tintoretto's early works, in the hypothetical production of the early 1540's, the Venetian influence was always pre-eminent; his native heritage resisted the influence of the time and personal likings. Titian made him ripe to absorb the art of Rome and Florence.

The Titian of the 1530's, whose pupil he was at all events for some time, could not carry him any further in this direction. But about 1540 Titian had undergone a transformation, perhaps partly caused by the same motives which acted upon Tintoretto, which brought him nearer to the pathetic, the heroic, the monumentally plastic, with his Crown of Thorns in Paris, his ceiling-paintings in the Salute, his John the Baptist in the Accademia, his Ecce Homo in Vienna, etc. This example of Titian's in the 1540's smoothed the way for Tintoretto, who was experimenting in the same direction; it showed him how to absorb the strange and unaccustomed elements without renouncing Venetian colouring. The fact that Titian showed him the way to Michelangelo gives Tintoretto's Miracle of St. Mark and its contemporary, the Miracle of St. Agnes *Figs. 27, 21* in Madonna dell'Orto, their chromatic brilliance and gaiety; this was not a mere creation out of the medium of colour—and the admirers of Titian recognized the heresy very clearly, as is shown by Aretino's mild words of blame—but a plastic and spatial construction by means of this glorious and sumptuous colouring. Thus Titian and Michelangelo balance each other in these works in a very curious manner.

Until this Tintoretto had occasionally turned to Titian, as if defiantly *Influence of* and against his will; now he abandoned himself more willingly to his natural *Titian* bent. The Miracle of St. Mark is not the only picture which shows the great extent of this approachement: the Miracle of St. Agnes also is indebted to Titian's Ecce Homo of 1543 in numerous details—for example, the blond-

Fig. 26   bearded horseman behind the kneeling Saint; the St. Martial in the church of
San Marciliano is a variation of Titian's St. John Elemosynarius, and the 1551
Fig. 31   Cain and Abel from the Trinità is a paraphrase of Titian's ceiling-paintings
in the Salute. In the Fall of Man in the same series, the Central Italian plastic
form transformed under Titian's influence and the painteresque landscape are
reconciled by the phenomenon of light. The master who created this coloured
Fig. 28   fable of the primitive world with a third picture in the same series, the Creation
of the Animals, did not sit as a pupil beneath the ceiling of the Sistina. In
all his transformations and phases of development he remained faithful to his
Venetian heritage.

This fundamental derivation from Venetian art is Tintoretto's essential
characteristic. Just as he worked almost exclusively for his native city and
furnished to customers from elsewhere almost invariably works of the second
rank—signed atelier paintings, such as he considered good enough for such
clients—with the result that even to-day Venice possesses the lion's share of
his work as regards both quality and quantity, whereas with Titian the contrary
is the case, so too Tintoretto never overstepped the artistic boundaries of
Venice. All the same, his attitude to the city's artistic tradition underwent
several transformations. Even before the beginning of his mature middle period
two phases can be distinguished. In the first—down to about 1548—he made
a naive attempt to analyse all that the broad stream of average artistic achievement brought him, without any dominant thread to guide him and ignoring
the chief factor, the work of Titian. Only when the revelation of the latter
came to him, at the same time fructifying the inspiration drawn from Central
Italian sources, did Tintoretto become more sure of himself and his strength
in his attitude to the artistic aims of his native city. His enhanced power of
conception was now able to achieve a fruitful union between opposing elements.
In the 1550's he turned to Florentine and Roman models. In the Pietà in the
Figs. 118, 141   Accademia the influence of Daniele da Volterra's much lauded Deposition in
the Trinità dei Monti has long been recognized, and this influence can be felt
also in the Entombment at Bridgewater House; the same painter's " Mercury's
message to Aeneas " (from a Swedish private collection, reproduced by Voss
in Kunstchronik, new series XXXIII, 376) was the forerunner of Tintoretto's
Vulcan picture at Munich. The almost acrobatic seated postures of the
Figs. 51, 52, 56   Evangelists in Santa Maria Zobenigo (after 1552) show reminiscences of Pelle-
grino Tibaldi's ceiling-paintings in the Palazzo Poggi, Bologna, executed shortly
before. Almost at the same time Tintoretto painted his pictures for the
Figs. 48, 49   Camerlenghi, in which he comes perceptibly nearer to Bonifazio than in his
youthful works. The antinomy between the penetration of Titian's influence
and the beginning of his study of Michelangelo leads him into deeper waters;
from a mighty extension in two opposite directions springs Tintoretto's own
style in its first phase.

Personal style   In it there found place the new dominant factors of movement and light,
the combination of which made the sought-after synthesis of form and colour

possible. Plastic form lives on only in movement, and even if it appears to be motionless, it is only in relationship to the pictorial whole; in the same way, colour loses its separate existence and it is lighting which now moulds the masses of the composition. Form and colour are no longer artistic aims in themselves or dominant principles of style; their dethronement aroused the disapproval of the leading theoreticians of both tendencies. Vasari, who otherwise appreciated every form of devotion to Michelangelo, used the strongest words in his condemnation of this dangerous genius "who works in a random way and without draughtsmanship, as if he wanted to show that his art is nothing but a joke;" and Aretino, who had been one of the defenders of the much-discussed Miracle of St. Mark, frowned upon the carelessness which he held could be excused only by the youth of the master. Aretino was no friend of broad brushwork, and its presence in his own portrait by Titian he explained as due to the unwillingness of his miserly friend to take trouble for so little money. In addition to this, what Aretino disliked in Tintoretto's colouring was the fact that, despite its fullness, it was not the real aim requiring all the artist's concentration, devotion and worship. It was not Titian's colouring, not so much as regards quality, but as being the medium and aim of painting. "The finest colours can be bought ready-made at the Rialto", was Tintoretto's retort.

The self-confidence thus achieved permeates all the pictures he painted during the 1550's. They are less problematic than is usual in his work. Thode formed the (erroneous) opinion that Tintoretto must have drawn the inspiration for his Rescue of Arsinoë from Greek mythology, but in reality it was a late antique Roman legend. A similarly naïve sensuousness is prevalent in other pictures—both sacred and profane—painted about this time, for example the Old Testament scenes from the Scuola della Trinità, the legend of St. George in London, the Paris Susanna, the Tiburtine Sibyl with Augustus, the pictures of Saints for the Camerlenghi. It is perhaps for this reason that during this period—and during this period only—Tintoretto painted mythological subjects of an unsophisticated objectivity which is otherwise absent from his works: the Leda in Florence, the Danaë in Lyons, the Venus and Vulcan in Munich, which I thus prefer to date from the 1550's, against the opinion of other writers. How much the artist strove in these pictures to give the impression of reality is confirmed by the compositional study in Berlin, the oldest and almost the only drawing of this kind by Tintoretto. Even in the portraits of this period we notice a happy easing of tension, a care-free abandonment; only in the portrait of the artist as a young man—if the picture in the Victoria & Albert Museum can rightly be described as such—do we find a flicker of the visionary flame which a generation later fills the self-portrait of the old artist with so weird a light.

The personal style which was to determine Tintoretto's mature period begins to take form at the end of the 1550's in these works drawn from so many sources; he concentrates all his energy on the achievement of more

Mythological subjects

Fig. 64

Figs. 28-31, coloured plate, 59, 70, 48, 49

Figs. 57, 60, 56, 55

Fig. 1

Figs. 98, 97 pathetic expression: the Presentation of the Virgin in Madonna dell'Orto—
together with the closely related Presentation in the Temple in the Accademia—
Figs. 117, 118, colour plate the Crucifixion from San Severo, the Mourning for the Body of Christ beneath
the Cross, and together with these dramatic conflicts between light and darkness,
the exaltation of light in the Vienna Susanna, where the light, irradiated by
the gleaming body of a woman, fills the fairy-like garden with sunlight,
creates bodies, builds up depth, conjures up brilliance, atmosphere and mystery.

Fig. 98 End of the early period The Presentation of the Virgin is one of the pictures which even Vasari
appreciated; the heroic proportions of the figures and the imaginative con-
ception seem to have impressed him as being in accordance with the times. The
general arrangement, however, is Venetian. Titian, whose own version of the
theme is so different, had exploited in the Pesaro Madonna the contrast
between one gently rising side and one steeply falling side of a pyramidal
construction turned sideways; Tintoretto heightens the dramatic effect by
lighting one side and leaving the other in the shadow. The aim of the picture
is the exaltation of the child Virgin, thrown into prominence by the three
groups of women with their children, while the steps glittering with gold set
off her shy little figure; her movement is interrupted once again by the obelisk
immediately before the zenith formed by the figures of the priests. This is also
the apex where the other leg of the triangle converges, the row of men on the
steps plunged in material darkness and spiritual twilight, fantastically muffled
or exposed; they are genre figures and at the same time symbols, for which
reason they are genuinely Tintorettesque and at the same time akin to the
contemporary Florentine artists such as Rosso, who, like Tintoretto, saw in the
emphasizing of material phenomena a means of creating spirituality. The
Renaissance affirmed and achieved reality both in life and in art. The period
which followed it endeavoured to discern in this dominated reality an image
of metaphysical essence.

III

THE STYLE OF TINTORETTO'S LAST YEARS

THE MIDDLE STYLE of an artist such as that from which we have tried to deduce the essentials of Tintorettos treatment of form means middle not only in regard to time but also in regard to conception. The term thus comprises the line of ideological development resulting from the sum total of the artist's works, a line to which the individual works approximate only in a comparative degree, and it does not denote merely the period of masculine maturity lying between youth and old age, though it is true that during this period the artist generally approaches most closely to the middle line. During this period the two conflicting forces, his need for individual expression and the general trend, come nearest to achieving perfect balance, because the artist now feels himself more in harmony with the prevailing opinions of his own generation than either before or afterwards. In his youth his individuality develops without the discipline of important and regular commissions, while in his old age the contrast between the constant claims upon his activities and the increasing isolation of a great master produces a tension, the tragic side of which I endeavoured to describe in an earlier volume when discussing the intrinsic perfection and out-of-dateness of Titian's style in his last years.

With Tintoretto a fundamentally similar process takes place—a division of his works into indifferent workshop productions and incomparable masterpieces of his old age—but not in so pronounced a sense, because the artist was socially and culturally closer to the class of people for whom he worked; in addition to this, through his already mentioned passion for securing commissions—which was very different from Titian's much-blamed acquisitiveness—he made himself the undisputed master of the works he executed. In the wealthy and respected Scuola di San Rocco we find him imposing his artistic personality so successfully, despite opposition at the beginning, that the decoration of the magnificent rooms at length became the most personal of all his works, the monument to his own art which it took him all his life to erect.

It is no exaggeration to say that Tintoretto worked all his life for the Scuola di San Rocco, for we have documentary evidence that in 1549 he painted the first of his scenes from the legend of the titulary saint, St. Rochus ministering to sufferers from the Plague (see the notes in the Catalogue of this volume). But the closer relationship does not begin until later, after an offer of Titian in 1553 to paint a large picture for San Rocco had been shelved for reasons we do

Scuola di
San Rocco

not know. In 1564 a competition was held for a large ceiling-painting in the Albergo or hostel, the presentation of which Ridolfi has spun out into an amusing anecdote. While all the other artists invited to compete—Paolo Veronese, Andrea Schiavone, Giuseppe Salviati—kept to the conditions laid down and presented their designs on the date agreed upon, Tintoretto managed to *Fig. 122* smuggle a finished picture into the oval compartment of the ceiling and exploited the surprise effect thus achieved still further by offering his work to the Scuola gratis. The minutes of the meetings of the Scuola tell us that many of the members took offence at this incorrect behaviour and that it needed some diplomacy on the part of the heads of the School, who favoured Tintoretto, before the St. Rochus in Glory, which had been unveiled in such unusual circumstances, was accepted. Nevertheless in this way Tintoretto gained a firm footing and was entitled to consider himself the privileged painter of the Confraternity all the more because in the following year the membership which had been promised in 1549 was granted to him. In the same year, 1565, he put the seal on his position by the execution of the mighty Crucifixion in the Albergo, followed in 1566—67 by the remaining wall- and ceiling-paintings in this room and the completion of the decoration of the church. The two main rooms were left for another ten years in a state of emptiness and neglect, as is proved by several complaints made at the time; this may have induced Tintoretto to undertake a new offensive. In 1575 he executed without charge the middle ceiling-painting of the upper hall (The Brazen Serpent), and at the beginning of 1577, against reimbursement of his out-of-pocket expenses, two more large ceiling-paintings (Moses striking the Rock and the Gathering of Manna) in the same hall. A few months later he offered to complete the decoration of the ceiling on the same terms. The magnificence of this rich decoration must have made the walls look even barer and dirtier by comparison, and so, on September 23rd, 1577, Tintoretto made that suggestion, by accepting which (on November 2nd) the Brotherhood transformed their house into one of the most magnificent art monuments of Venice and Italy. The artist undertook, in return for a yearly stipend of one hundred ducats, to execute at his own expense all the pictures still required for the Scuola and the church. The agreement was faithfully kept by both parties. Tintoretto received his yearly stipend from the funds of the Brotherhood and painted between 1577 and 1581 all the wall-paintings of the upper hall (except the altar, which was executed subsequently in 1588), and between 1583 and 1587 those of the lower hall. The only thing which remained undone was the painting of a ceiling in the church suggested by Tintoretto in his original proposals.

This brief résumé of the history of the paintings in San Rocco is intended to show that Tintoretto here enjoyed an exceptional degree of independence; he was working not only for a community with whom he felt himself spiritually akin, but in consequence of the special circumstances he was working without competitors, without prescribed rules and without supervision. The small committee which examined the works delivered every year probably concerned itself more with the keeping of the agreement than with the quality of the separate works. Tintoretto worked here as if he were working for himself; it was granted to him to live out his full artistic life.

This does not mean that the choice of subjects was left entirely to him. In their subject-matter these wall- and ceiling-paintings represent such a thoughtful renovation of the typological system linking the events of the Old and New Testaments and such an original adaptation to the charitable purposes of the Confraternity as symbolized in the three chief pictures of the ceiling, that the programme can scarcely have been conceived without the collaboration of learned advisers. The programme presupposes not only a thorough knowledge of the Bible, but also a very subtle theological education, such as we can hardly believe Tintoretto possessed. What he himself contributed was the artistic moulding of the train of thought. The concordance of the ten mural scenes from the Life of Christ is a particularly characteristic example of this; they fit in with one another by reason of their content, and also with the ceiling-compartments above them, but they also belong together in pairs, one opposite the other, from the compositional point of view. The first group represents the Nativity of Christ and his Temptation by Satan; both the compositions are divided into two, with separate upper and lower parts; in the Nativity we have the animal warmth of the stable and the mysterious moment of the birth of the Holy Child watched over by the stars; in the Temptation, the demonic earthly power rising upwards and the divine grace descending from the mysterious thicket. The second pair are the overcrowded small-figure compositions, rising into depth, of the Baptism of Christ and the Miracle at the Pool of Bethesda, the third the two mighty pictures of the Resurrection and the Ascension, the latter with chains woven out of bodies which terminate at the upper edge of the picture in the soaring figure of the Saviour. The visionary element is emphasized still more by the large Apostle with the book, who is depicted as a witness of the miraculous event. After this come the two nocturnal scenes of the Agony in the Garden and the Raising of Lazarus, both of them again constructed on two levels, the action developing in the one case from bottom to top and in the other in the reverse direction. Lastly the Last Supper and the Miracle of the Loaves and Fishes, which with their subjects denoting spiritual and corporal nourishment have an obvious connection, but which have also similarities in their form, the compositions rising into depth, while the principal theme is thrust into the middle ground by the figures of the satiated in the foreground. This part of the great spiritual poem is thus narrated in five strophes.

Even so short a description as this of the paintings in the upper hall shows how varied were Tintoretto's conceptions and how carefully he avoids monotony of form. In the pictures painted a few years later in the lower hall the lack of sameness is even more noticeable. In this case each picture follows a different principle, each is filled with a different atmosphere and reveals different stylistic influences, although they were all executed about the same

Paintings in the upper hall Figs. 186-198

Figs. 200, 201

Figs. 204, 205
Figs. 202, 203

Figs. 206, 207

Figs. 208, 209

Paintings in the lower hall

Figs. 246-261 time. They seem to have nothing in common except the same directness and freedom of conception. This is due to the fact that here Tintoretto, as we remarked, above, was working so to speak for himself and at the same time for his fellow-members, with whose simple piety he had been familiar for years. It was to them that he narrated the lives of Christ and His Mother, taking pains to extract the deepest significance from each episode. The deliberateness of his representations is remote from that reformatory intention which Anglo-Saxon writers in particular have tried to deduce from them. If some of these pictures seem to depart from the tradition then prevailing, this is due not to a spirit of theological opposition, but on the contrary to the desire to reveal again the hitherto obscured original significance of the sacred stories. Because this return to the earliest sources also played an important part in the Reformation in Northern Europe, some writers have talked of a certain affinity between Tintoretto and that Reformation, reminding us that the attitude of the so-called Christian humanists or reformed Catholics in Italy about the middle of the century was similar to that prevailing in Germany before the Reformation. That one of the centres of this movement was in Venice itself, is well known; but we know nothing as to whether there were any links between its leading figures, Reginald Pole and Gasparo Contarini, and Tintoretto's spiritual advisers or the artist himself. We must content ourselves with noting that Tintoretto succeeded in extracting a similar deepening and renewal of the Christian subject-matter from a similar spiritual situation, as Dürer did; how far deliberate intention contributed to this, seems to us to be perhaps of less importance than the fact that both artists combined inimitable depth of temperament with unusual plastic power. Both of them depict their subjects in so penetrating a manner that it seems as if they were discovering for the first time matter which hitherto had never been treated.

Northern elements Figs. 246, 248, 252   This essential affinity between the two artists makes it tempting to assume a direct derivation of the younger from the older. In the construction of the spatial setting in the Annunciation or the Adoration or in the suggestive stormy landscape of the Flight into Egypt, some writers have thought to discern the influence of Dürer's graphics; but this influence can hardly have been a direct one from one work to another, but was more likely transmitted by the art of the period following upon Dürer, which was so strongly influenced by him. Throughout his life Tintoretto was an eager learner and among those who influenced him must be included not only the Venetian and Central Italian masters, but also the Northern Mannerists, who were accessible to him in reproductions; a borrowing of Heemskerk from Tintoretto has also been *Fig. 147* mentioned—the large angel in the picture of Limbo in San Cassiano painted in 1568—but the chronological situation is by no means certain, for the angel is found in an engraving by Heemskerk executed in 1563, and the Netherlandish artists who frequently appeared in Venetian ateliers must certainly have given as well as taken. Tintoretto did not avoid external influences, nor did he attempt to conceal them. In the Vulcan's Smithy in the Ducal Palace

he used a figure from a fresco by Signorelli at Orvieto; in the Massacre of the *Figs. 226, 258*
Innocents on the ground-floor of the Scuola di San Rocco he drew inspiration
from Giovanni da Bologna's relief of the Rape of the Sabines in Florence.
Tintoretto was no longer of an age to overrate the value of original conception;
in San Rocco he did not hesitate to use again a whole series of motifs drawn
from others.

Again and again one has the feeling that everything he painted in the *Spiritual conception*
Scuola di San Rocco was done according to the dictates of his own heart. The
great Crucifixion in the Sala dell'Albergo, painted in 1565, has already this *Folding plate*
completeness in the grandeur of the formal treatment and in the depth of the
spiritual conception; the moving spectacle of the lonely death upon the Cross
above a crowd of people engrossed in their own affairs is heightened by the
impressive grandeur of the scene, the intense vitality and the pathos which
permeates it in every sense. The Christ before Pilate and the Bearing of the *Figs. 200, 201*
Cross on the opposite wall are on the same high level. There is about all of
them something monumental, something which is authoritative in comparison
with the intimacy and fervour which the paintings on the walls of the two
other rooms breathe forth despite their great size. The very first pair
of pictures, the Adoration and the Temptation, are good examples of the
wonderful results which a combination of exactitude and mysticism, so
characteristic of the Catholic revival at this time, could produce from out of
the creative fantasy of a great artist. Note how in the first picture the
earthly is transformed into the animal element, in order to make the divine
birth still more sacred; or how in the second it rises to joyful pride in order
to render the divine victory more striking. In the heroic representation of
the Tempter Tintoretto returns to Byzantine tradition, which adorned the
Prince of Evil with all the seductive glitter of outward appearance; in
moulding the head after one of the Medici heads which he had studied so *Figs. 213, 214*
attentively, Tintoretto found the best possible means of achieving the ideal.

Lack of space prevents us from dealing one by one with the cycle of
pictures on the walls of the two rooms. Ruskin's and Thode's analysis of the
individual works have retained enough of their original clear-sightedness and
warmth to serve as guides, even to-day. Even without them the spectator who
remembers similar cycles by other artists will be able without difficulty to
appreciate its special qualities. These are derived from the new consciousness
of personal religious experience. Those who are familiar with the religious
history of the sixteenth century know the importance which this attitude
possessed for the leading personalities of the time—St. Ignatius of Loyola or
St. Theresa—and how deep was its influence on all subsequent developments.
Various modern writers have attempted to investigate these analogies drawn
from religious history in their relationship to Tintoretto's art; we may content
ourselves with the statement that the incomparable freshness and wealth of
experience in his pictorial visions found their counterparts in the features of
the religious innovators. For him too life was a struggle; peace was to be

found only in the beyond, and this conviction fills all his paintings with an atmosphere of acute suspense—whether the scenes are dramatic or lyrical in mood, the Resurrection or the Agony in the Garden, the Massacre of the Innocents or the Flight into Egypt. Only the two female hermit-saints, whom most of the older describers of this series usually overlooked, enjoy the peace of the life to come: St. Mary Aegyptiaca, turning away from the spectator towards infinity, and St. Mary Magdalen, absorbed in her book and far from every other thought of this world; both are small figures, tiny in comparison with the gigantic trees which overshadow them, dissolved into the dreamlike landscape, with the twilight peace of which the tempestuousness of the other pictures is in harmony.

Figs. 202, 206, 258, 247

Figs. 260, 261

The undogmatic profession of faith in these lay sermons has its counterpart in the style, aiming decisively at effect; the treatment of form in the San Rocco pictures was also influenced by the exceptional and unique circumstances of their creation. These works, created for the edification of Tintoretto himself and of those who held the same convictions, were painted for rooms the unfavourable lighting conditions of which were known and deplored by all of us until the installation of clever lighting apparatus and reflectors on the occasion of the Mostra in 1937. Here an indulgence in refinements of colour would have been superfluous; here a broad brushwork was indicated, a powerful treatment of light setting off the masses in the pictures. Here the monumental style, which inner reasons demanded, was bound, for external reasons also, to lead to a simplification of the compositions, to a reduction to types of the figures and to a generalization of heads and features. All this contributes to the impression of unreality which the pictures produce. It makes these visions irresistible and eliminates all necessity for pictorial refinements.

The " San Rocco " style

The part which the work for the Scuola di San Rocco played in Tintoretto's activities, especially after 1577, inevitably had a decisive influence on the style of his late period; it was a foundation upon which the style of his old age, with its self-sufficiency and regardlessness, could freely unfold itself. It becomes Tintoretto's last and most personal expression even in works painted for other buildings: the Washing of Feet or the Agony in the Garden in San Stefano, the St. Michael and Satan now in Dresden, the legend of St. Catherine from Santa Caterina, all kinds of sketchy and unfinished works which give the impression that they were created to satisfy a thirst for creation rather than to comply with the wishes of those who commissioned them. Nevertheless there is no mutually exclusive contrast between these two urges to creation, for they summarize the unity of Tintoretto's artistic personality; in addition to this it is certain that even in San Rocco not everything was left to the discretion of the artist. A certain constraint is perceptible in the ceiling-paintings of the Sala dell'Albergo and the upper hall; on the one hand, these works were created between 1565 and 1567, that is to say before Tintoretto had obtained full sway over the Scuola, and on the other hand the connection between

Figs. 267, 266, 268, 280

pictorial content and decoration must here have been a hindrance to the freedom of fantasy. The not very varied episodes from the stories of the Old Testament Prophets could not call forth a passionate participation of feeling, as the scenes from the Passion or the life of the Virgin could do. Nevertheless we are bound to admire the happy way in which Tintoretto mastered these arid subjects; the three great pictures of Moses with which he began his regular *Figs. 186-196* work for the Scuola are not the only ones which must be counted among his finest conceptions; even in the oval compartments with their sameness of subjects he is always original and fertile. The Fall of Man and the Paschal Feast, the Jacob's Ladder and Elisha feeding the People show to an equal degree the artist's participation in the conception; but they might lead us to suppose, so far as it is possible to form any opinion after the extensive restoration undertaken by Giuseppe Angeli in 1778, that Tintoretto's share in the execution was smaller. Nevertheless he must have regarded even these ceiling-paintings as his own personal concern.

Others who commissioned Tintoretto to paint works had more definite *Works for the* ideas of their own. All the time he was engaged in painting for the Scuola *Ducal Palace* di San Rocco, Tintoretto was also working for the Ducal Palace and other public buildings, and what he did in this way for the State was not inferior in quantity to the works he executed for the Scuola. In fact at certain times Tintoretto was overwhelmed with orders and it has been suggested that the abundance of such commissions may have been the explanation of the pause in his activity for the Scuola di San Rocco between 1567 and 1575. Of the pictures he painted at that time many, and among them some of the most important, were destroyed in the fires at the Ducal Palace in 1574 and 1577, though what he painted after 1580 to replace the burnt pictures has been for the most part preserved. The catastrophe forms a dividing line, not only in external factors, between two different periods of production.

Before the fires Tintoretto had time and tranquillity enough to create personal solutions of the various tasks. The ceiling-painting in the Atrio Quadrato showing Doge Girolamo Priuli receiving the sword of his exalted *Fig. 90* office from Justice and Venetia in the presence of his patron saint, is a pleasing conception despite the general allegorical nature of the subject, and its warm colouring is well suited to the magnificence of the architectural setting. Still more charming is the ceiling-decoration which has only quite recently been restored to its original position in the Sala degli Inquisitori; the middle picture of the Parable of the Prodigal Son, with its expressive *Figs. 74, 73* silhouettes and discreet colouring, has resemblances too and was painted at about the same time as other works from the 1560's—the Invention of the Cross or the Deposition in Caën. The drawing in the Uffizi, which may be *Figs. 87, 142* assumed to be the first draft of the idea, with the looseness with which the elements of its composition are bound together, shows that these early decorative works for public buildings were created without the workshop routine which can be discerned in later works of this kind. In the case of the

Figs. 160-164 Philosophers for the main hall of Sansovino's Library Tintoretto must have been spurred on by the rivalry with certain other artists; those which were allotted to him show the efforts he made to surpass the merits of the others by the bold, sometimes deliberate vivacity of his figures, in contrast to the dignified distinction of Paolo Veronese's figures. It has rightly been observed that these vivacious old men, the exuberance of their bodies wrapped in the poverty of their philosophers' robes, are the worldly counterparts of the Figs. 210, 211 Prophets in the Sala dell'Albergo and the two saintly healers of the plague in the upper hall of the Scuola di San Rocco; they belong to the race of spiritual warriors with whom the artist felt an inner affinity and whom he consequently painted with the improvising sureness of self-portraits.

"*The Battle of Lepanto*"   Tintoretto showed particular zeal in devoting himself to the painting of the Signoria's official picture commemorating the naval victory of Lepanto. The decision to have this painting executed was taken in 1572 and at first the intention seems to have been to entrust the order to the aged Titian, who was to be helped by Giuseppe Salviati; but as in the case of the San-Rocco ceiling, Tintoretto managed to obtain the order for himself by submitting a finished picture and making a present of it to the Signoria. When we remember the boundless rejoicing with which Venice greeted the news of the Christian fleet's victory over her traditional enemy, we can imagine Tintoretto's enthusiasm for the colossal task of depicting the great event with all its essential details and its leading figures; in his petition for the reversion of a broker's patent at the Fondaco, Tintoretto refers to this picture, stating that he worked on it for ten months and that his expenses alone, which he paid out of his own pocket, amounted to two hundred ducats, "because he had designed everything from nature." The large amount spent on models shows with what care he made his preparations; among the drawings of nudes in heroic attitudes which have been preserved and which have not yet been assigned to a definite place in Tintoretto's *œuvre*, many must certainly have been connected with the lost masterpiece. It was destroyed in the fire of 1577, and there is no reproduction which helps us to form an idea of it; there is only a Battle of Lepanto recently acquired by the Museo Correr and possibly connected with a second version, likewise destroyed by fire, which Tintoretto painted for SS. Giovanni e Paolo, to give us some idea of what a picture of a naval battle by Tintoretto looked like.

The substitute for the lost picture was executed by Andrea Vicentino in Tintoretto's lifetime, while to the latter were entrusted numerous other works for the redecoration of the Ducal Palace. We can imagine that he took far less interest in this mass-production, for at this time, in the 1580's, his activities at San Rocco must have absorbed most of his energies. The restoration of the Ducal Palace was undertaken with great energy and according to a uniform programme, which its authors have transmitted to us in detailed writings. This was the first time that art was used as an instrument of systematic propaganda on behalf of the state and its institutions, a novelty which later had its influence on Baroque art. The resulting general impression is undoubtedly one of magnificence, but an artist of Tintoretto's quality can hardly have felt himself attracted by these stereotyped glorifications of Venice and her rulers; the general opinion nowadays is that to these extensive decorations of his late period he contributed only the conception—and that perhaps often only to a limited degree—and the collaboration of his workshop.

Before this mass-production began, Tintoretto had already painted several *Decorative* masterpieces which give a direct idea of his "Ducal Palace style," if it is *paintings* permissible to coin such an expression as a contrast to his "San Rocco style." These are the allegorical ceiling-paintings in the Atrio, the four mythological *Figs. 225-228,* pictures which in the eighteenth century were transferred from another part *177* of the palace to the said room, and the closely related Luna and the Horae from the Fondaco dei Tedeschi, now in the Kaiser-Friedrich-Museum, Berlin. All these works were painted between 1577 and 1580, the period of Tintoretto's greatest activity at San Rocco, and form a marked contrast with the works he painted there. Once again Tintoretto demonstrates his faculty of adapting himself to the special requirements of a task. In contrast to what had been the case at San Rocco, he had now to satisfy a public of fastidious art-lovers by offering them careful execution, harmony with an exuberant architectural setting, and ingenious renderings of captious conceptions. At San Rocco Tintoretto was his own master, here he had to compete with masters of decorative effect—above all, with Paolo Veronese—and an approach to their style becomes noticeable about this time. The mighty surge of his compositions at San Rocco is here transformed into a pleasant and attractive melodiousness, the fundamental importance of which for Tintoretto's style will be discussed later. He had also to adapt himself to the subjects. That the mythological themes could not offer him much scope, is only natural; they could only be filled out with subtle references excogitated by a literary mind. The four pictures in the Atrio Quadrato, the gracefulness of which is so unaffected that we have no time to think of their significance, symbolize the wisdom of Venetian administration. Ridolfi explains to us what Bacchus and Ariadne, Minerva and Mars, the three Graces and Mercury and Vulcan's Smithy signify in this connection; and this programme was not attributed subsequently to the pictures, for in the payment entry of November 10th, 1578, it is expressly stated that the four pictures together symbolize unity.

This ability to adapt himself to the ideas of those who gave him *Battle pictures* commissions is surprising in the eyes of a later generation for whom art has *for Mantua* become the unrestrained expression of creative individuality, but in Tintoretto's time it was perfectly normal. We can consult the correspondence between him and the agent of the Mantuan government concerning the eight pictures which he painted in 1579-80 and which are now in the Pinakothek *Figs. 220-224* at Munich; for each of the eight scenes from the history of the Gonzagas he received a detailed programme, and the designs which he had to submit were subjected to a meticulous criticism as to their objective exactitude—the position

of a battery in a battle, the lifelikeness of the portraits, the faithful reproduction of costumes—before he was allowed to proceed with the execution;
nevertheless the latter is as vivid as if nothing had hampered the unrestricted
Fig. 219
Figs. 233, 234 fantasy of the artist. In fact, among Tintoretto's sketches for these pictures we
have only one drawing in Naples which in vigour and ingenuity is far superior
to the finished picture. The same may be said of the New York design for
the votive picture of Doge Alvise Mocenigo, the execution of which in the
Sala del Collegio at the Ducal Palace is a thoroughly conventional atelier
Fig. 244,
folding plate product. The design for the Paradise in the Sala del Gran Consiglio has
likewise been preserved (in Paris); it was submitted by Tintoretto in 1579 on
the occasion of the competition for this picture; the deviations, which at the
same time are changes for the worse, in the finished painting are so considerable—and moreover so very much in accordance with the designs submitted
by the other competitors, Veronese, Bassano and Palma—that it is permissible
to attribute them to the pressure of the authorities. It is not surprising that
Tintoretto should have left to his assistants the execution of a painting which
had been deprived of the vigour of its conception. Moreover the painting
was executed so long after the design, that the great age of the master alone must
have prevented him from working intensively on it.

Workshop
procedure   The great importance of artist's workshops in Venice is deeply rooted
in the social and cultural structure of the city. As early as the fifteenth
century the Vivarini and Bellini carried on their work as family businesses.
In the sixteenth century the large ateliers were organized entirely on this
basis; after the death of Veronese, his sons, his brother and his nephew carried
on the business under the style of "the heirs of Paul," while about the same
time the Bassani enlarged their business by availing themselves of the services
of other members of the family on the largest possible scale. Similar arrangements in Titian's workshop have been overlooked, to the great detriment of
the proper understanding of his art. Tintoretto, too, had an efficient workshop
at his disposal from the beginning; as soon as his children were old enough,
they were given privileged positions in the atelier, and Domenico in particular
became his father's foreman and agent. In his will Jacopo laid down that
Domenico was to complete the unfinished works in the same way and manner
as he had done previously with many of Jacopo's pictures, and expresses the
desire that Marco too, the less favoured son, should remain a member of the
firm. The children continued to consider the practice of art as a family
business; when Domenico's pupil Sebastiano Casser asked Domenico's sister
Ottavia to marry him, she gave her consent on the condition that he should
prove himself to be a good painter, stipulating that she would not marry him
until he had become an efficient member of the family undertaking.

These patriarchal notions form the background of the extensive activity
of Tintoretto's workshop, the backbone of which was the exploitation of the
available stock of drawings, plaster casts, models and other accessories.
Tintoretto stipulated in his will that to begin with everything should be kept

SALA DEL GRAN CONSIGLIO, with Tintoretto's " Paradise ". Venice, Ducal Palace.

ROOM ON THE UPPER STOREY OF THE SCUOLA DI SAN ROCCO, with Tintoretto's wall and ceiling paintings. Venice.

PLATE VII

CARICATURE OF TINTORETTO. Wood carving by Francesco Pianta il Giovane. Venice, Scuola di San Rocco.

together; Domenico bequeathed to Casser four casts, of which one was a head of Vitellius and another a full-length figure, and a large number of drawings, from which he was free to choose for himself 150 male and fifty female studies from life, as well as other workshop materials. As late as the eighteenth century the accessories of Tintoretto's workshop could still be seen for the greater part together; even nowadays, the number of drawings of very unequal quality from the same models, for example the above-mentioned head of Vitellius—which had also been a favourite accessory of Titian's workshop—show that artistic education based on the same material and the same principles was obviously considered an important factor for achieving uniformity among the members of the atelier.

The working arrangements in Tintoretto's atelier were somewhat different from those in Titian's. Whereas in the latter the pupils made replicas which were merely repetitions of a model with few variations, in Tintoretto's workshop such repetitions were almost entirely lacking. Instead of them we have remodellings and enlargements. The Nativity of John the Baptist in the Hermitage is an amplified version of the picture of the same subject in San Zaccaria, Venice; the Christ in the House of the Pharisee at the Escorial stands in the same relation to the version in the Museo Civico at Padua, the Samson and Delilah in the Duke of Devonshire's collection is similarly related to the more compact version in the Ringling Museum, Sarasota (Florida). Hadeln, who assembled these examples, draws attention to the fact that in the Leningrad version of the Nativity the principal group of the San Zaccaria picture is shown in reverse. This was one of the devices employed by the workshop to multiply the number of models. The workshop repetition of the Woman taken in Adultery at the Prado reverses Tintoretto's composition in Dresden in all essential details, while the St. Jerome in Vienna is a reversal of one of the Philosophers in the Libreria at Venice. Isolated drawings by Tintoretto are likewise reversed, or else the outlines are retained, but the figures seen from behind instead of from the front; while in other cases only the draperies or other accessories are altered. The drawing in the Königs collection, originally used for a figure in the Oxford Martyrdom of St. Lawrence, was used a second time in the so-called Rape of Helen in the Prado. Drawings, and especially those studies from the nude in which with feverish haste and unfailing accuracy he defined elementary or complicated attitudes and movements, seem to have been the chief means employed by Tintoretto to influence the work of his assistants. But he must also have used complete designs for those compositions the execution of which was left to the workshop; and in addition to the drawings—such as the newly-discovered sketch for the "Battle on the Taro" at Munich—we may suppose that painted models also existed. From what we know of Domenico's procedure, about which the album in London—originally supposed to be Jacopo's, but now for adequate reasons attributed to his son—gives us plenty of information, we may assume that the practice in his father's atelier was similar. The large sketches painted on canvas for the

Tintoretto's workshop

Fig. 4

Fig. 2

Figs. 169, 245

Fig. 219

Figs. 234, 244

votive picture of Doge Alvise Mocenigo (in the Metropolitan Museum) and for the Paradise in the Ducal Palace (at the Louvre) differ so markedly from the paintings executed by the workshop that they must be assumed to be general sketches or models submitted to those who commissioned the works rather than working models for the use of those who actually did the painting. In addition to this Tintoretto may have made quick sketches of ideas for pictures, like those abbozzi which he had seen and admired in Titian's atelier; the Crown of Thorns (now in Munich) was acquired by Tintoretto from among the abbozzi left by Titian after his death. Something of the gifted recklessness of *Figs. 243, 108* such models can be detected in Tintoretto's Vienna Flagellation or in the fragment of the Muses in the Lanz collection, Amsterdam, of which we have a complete version, executed by the workshop, at Hampton Court.

In any case there were various means by which the master could exercise influence over his workshop. He used his own works to educate his assistants, until their manner of seeing and depicting approximated to his own; he guided them by means of sketches and designs, placed his own drawings at their disposal, and made them draw similar motifs from similar models; he taught them how to combine all these elements so as to form a general Tintorettesque style. The latter is not the personal style of Tintoretto, but it encloses it as the violin-case encloses the violin, roughening all the lines, but yet following them. The Tintorettesque style is not only an impoverishment, but also an enrichment of the style of Tintoretto; it enters into innumerable combinations with the personal style, makes transitions and mixtures possible, increases the master's scope, augments his effectiveness, and affords opportunity for trying out on a larger scale artistic principles which in reality are his own personal property.

Tintoretto's last style and school works   We must bear this polarity in mind if we are to do justice to the individuality of Tintoretto—especially in the years of his later maturity; between what is really his in the narrower and broader senses of the term there lie hundreds of graduations which make it impossible to judge his works by the standard of whether he himself had a greater or a smaller share in their execution. Works in which pupils certainly had a considerable share—as for *Figs. 274, 275* instance the two mighty late works in San Giorgio Maggiore—are among his most important and most personal creations; in others—like the similarly *Figs. 281, 282* ambitious pictures in the choir of San Trovaso—the balance between what is his and what is not makes us hesitate. Even among the portraits we find some which belong to this category of mixed products. Our current conceptions have made us too ready to regard works of this kind as the offspring of an individual will to create, and to overlook the fact that in the Cinquecento they were the standard stock-in-trade, the everyday productions of workshops. The importance of the sitter, or artistic interest in his appearance, conditions of payment, the amount of leisure and other circumstances determined the proportions of the shares taken by the master and the assistants in such cases— and this is true of other products as well. In portraiture Domenico was his father's right hand; and his brother-in-law Sebastian Casser is specifically mentioned as the portrait specialist of the atelier. It is significant that not a single example of his much-lauded talent for portraiture is known, and we must conclude that it has disappeared in the depths of the Tintorettesque style. Moreover, for Tintoretto the portrait was not, as it was for Titian, an independent branch of painting equal in value to all other branches, but more intimately connected with his treatment of other themes; its development out of sacred art—an essential component in the origins of portraits as a whole— takes place in the case of Tintoretto, the simpler and more craftsmanlike artist, under our very eyes.

Portraits of donors have a disproportionately large place in Tintoretto's work. He inserted the conceited Tommaso Rangoni as an active participator in the Miracles of St. Mark,—in 1573 the Scuola di San Marco, while the donor was still alive, wanted to eliminate these too personal tributes and sent the pictures back to Tintoretto for that purpose in the autumn of that year. Michele Bon appears in the beautiful late picture in San Giuseppe di Castello, as prominent as a patron saint, and in the Christ in Limbo in San Cassiano the donors are mingled with the other sinners who await salvation. The inter-mingling, usual in Venice, of official and religious life had this consequence that in official portraits Doges were promoted to the ranks of the heavenly household, while saints condescend to intimate intercourse with functionaries of lesser rank; three Camerlenghi, accompanied by their servants, bow humbly before the Madonna, other treasury officials kneel reverently before St. Mark (Berlin) or St. Justina (Venice). Among the painters of the preceding generation, Bonifazio—imitated by Tintoretto in isolated pictures—painted only the patron saints of the donors on similar occasions, and at the most inserted the donor's coat-of-arms. Now the donors themselves make their appearance, but they are conscious of the distinction conferred upon them, and their inward emotion betrays that they feel themselves to be in the presence of holy protectors. Something of this emotion is found in Tintoretto's figures, even if they are not accompanied by saints, and this inspired feeling seems to me to be the hall-mark of his portraits, in comparison with those created according to similar prin-ciples of painting by Domenico and other assistants and imitators. It is as if a reflection and consciousness of a higher existence had enveloped them in their everyday life. In his earlier years this characteristic is often—but not always— lost owing to the influence of Titian or other form; he strives to give his models a certain charm and pleasingness, which eclipses their simple humanity. Later this spiritual element becomes stronger and stronger. Not in the sense that the external accessories are treated with less care—that depends solely on the rank of the sitter and the purpose of the picture—but the proportion and impression of humanity becomes more and more direct. Not only what the sitter is, but how he is, becomes relatively unimportant, his representative and psychological value evaporate into baubles, measured in these pictures by the warm wave of humanity—in the sense of adoption by God. With works of

Portraits

Figs. 111-113

Figs. 269, 143

*Figs. 232, 233,
156, 274*

this kind we must consider it certain that they were painted by his hand, whereas the contrary was the case with his above-mentioned official portraits. But even within this narrow circle of choice, it has recently been shown that the picture of the old man with his grandson in the Vienna gallery, a work highly praised by writers, was possibly painted by his daughter Marietta, though it is true that she had her father to guide her hand.

Fig. 153

Tintoretto and Marietta

Tintoretto's special relationship to his daughter, who was bodily and spiritually his creation, is only a curious instance of his ability to make his workshop the receptacle and instrument of his artistic will. Its custom, described above, of disintegrating the elements received from him, remoulding them and re-arranging them by means of reversal and combination, is the outward expression of a process which he himself followed in his own creative work. What we defined when discussing his "middle style" as the depreciation of form and colour, is logically developed in the late period. The colours, deprived of their relationship to the subject and of the intention to provide sensual attraction, are applied side by side in well-defined patches, and from the clashing juxtaposition of these patches there springs a rhythm which can best be compared with that of mosaics. Parenthetically it should be noted

Fig. 171

here that Tintoretto had a large share in the decoration of St. Mark's and that he and Domenico made numerous cartoons for mosaics. Attempts have been made to prove that with Titian too the disintegration of colour in the style of his old age was due to his busying himself with, and gaining instruction from, this Venetian branch of art; but with him the intention and effect are entirely different from what they were with Tintoretto. Through their decomposition, toning down and juxtaposition, Titian's colours are intended to begin to play, and to create out of their own selves a vision of the material and spiritual world; Tintoretto's colours are not intended to play, their coldness makes them rigid, they remain multicoloured patches, from which the specially favoured tones break out rather than bloom forth. In the large pictures in Madonna dell'Orto or the Legend of St. Roch we see the preparation of this

Figs. 270, 274, 275, 283

process; in late works like the Christ in the house of Martha and Mary, at Munich, the Baptism of Christ in San Silvestro, and above all in the large wide pictures and the Deposition in Santa Maggiore, we find it in its completed form.

Transformation of colour and form

A transformation of form runs parallel with this transformation of colour. The excessive importance attached to the single figures in the very early period, which are later incorporated in the current of movement of the composition, does not disappear completely even in the latest works. The figures retain their value and significance in so far as they are noticeable elements in the pictorial construction. But they are subordinated more than in the early pictures to the prevailing rhythm; moreover they are arbitrarily repeated, varied, and shifted. In the hands of the assistants this sometimes results in an artificial mechanism, but in those of the master it becomes a means for achieving innumerable effects. Motives of posture and movement are strewn like accents over the picture, direct or reversed, driving or restraining forces are balanced, the crowding together or dispersal of masses developed contrapunctally. In large compositions—whether executed by the master's own hand or with the help of pupils—certain motives are repeated and modified, as for example the man falling with his arms stretched out in front of him in the Battle on the Adige; this repetition with variants of the same fundamental form is what gives the driving force to the rhythm of these pictures. Almost all scholars who have sought to define the essential features of Tintoretto's style have drawn analogies from music; they have pointed to the old kinship between music and painting in Venice and noted that Tintoretto secured the services of the most famous virtuoso of his time as music-teacher for his daughter, while he himself is said to appear among the members of the orchestra of artists which is found in one of Paolo Veronese's magnificent feasts. A later writer has even tried to draw from Vasari's statement that Tintoretto loved music above all the other fine arts, and could play several instruments, the deduction that Vasari too considered its musicality to be the dominant quality in Tintoretto's art. The passage in question, which refers more to his secondary artistic activities, does not justify such a sweeping assertion, but it may unconsciously express a deep intuition. Tintoretto's artistic expression, especially the style of his old age in its phase of freedom from external pressure, can best be defined by an analogy with music.

Musical element

In the late works a free formal intention develops according to its own laws; all desire to reproduce nature and all regard for the subject represented seem to have been eliminated, except perhaps that the subject determines the choice of key. Invention streams forth with a light and pleasing touch in the Berlin picture of Diana, in the Madonna with Saints Cosmas and Damian in the Accademia, in the Temptation of St. Anthony in San Trovaso; in wild pathos in the Martyrdom of St. Catherine, in the Rape of Helen or the St. Michael and Satan in Dresden. In the first three pictures nothing seems to disturb the harmony; in the last three harmony liberates itself from the convulsions and struggles of conflicting forces. This last style reaches its highest pinnacle in the pictures in San Giorgio Maggiore. In the Last Supper Tintoretto turns again to the subject which accompanied him like a main theme throughout his life as an artist. Never before had he achieved such a distance from the material facts as in this solemn, mysterious picture, in which the interior, spiritualized by the heavenly messengers, stretches to infinity, while an open semicircle of episodic supernumerary personages, in the other half of the picture, is placed before the block formed by the figures of the Apostles seated at the brightly lighted table running into depth. In contrast to the sorrowful emotion of this picture we have the gay lightness of the Gathering of Manna; groups and single figures are strewn about the pictorial planes; Moses, seated in the right foreground, is linked by the old man pointing behind him with a whole world, in which everything takes place according to the rules of everyday life, despite the fact that the laws of nature seem to have been

Figs. 177, 175, 176, 280, 245, 268

Fig. 275

Fig. 274

Fig. 283

suspended. The normal laws of statics have no value here, and what actually happens in the picture recedes entirely into the background; at all events it is not the intention of the composition to render it more intelligible. When we stand before the Entombment, with its direct appeal to the heart—painted for the same church and perhaps in the year of Tintoretto's death—we feel still more clearly that the gruesome and tragic event is taking place behind the veil of a formal play of line and colour.

This withdrawal of the objective element from relation with reality to a higher spiritual sphere has the same sobering effect as many other features of the manneristic period. For us, the heirs of a naturalistic conception, it is difficult to understand that contemporary students of art, as we know from numerous literary testimonies, considered this spiritualization a deepening and strengthening of effect, and approved it. But the interest in manneristic art, which in our own time is increasing so markedly, shows on the other hand that this transference of the spiritual element to the sphere specially suited to it is not fundamentally inaccessible to us. At the Tintoretto Mostra the late Entombment from San Giorgio filled us, almost like a greeting from beyond the tomb, with the sorrowful sweetness which the liberation of spiritually exalted events from the empiricism of reality always evokes. Still more we were impressed by Tintoretto's power of expression in the two pictures in wide format from the same church, which show the innermost mysticism of the Christian religion in the pure medium of art. In the one, the abundance of workaday life split up into innumerable episodes—craftsmen and housewives busy at their tasks—and as a contrast to these bodily needs, which through the words of the Lord's Prayer have become a part of religious consciousness, the appeasement of spiritual hunger by the bread and wine of the Eucharist. The deepest significance of the subject represented is displayed with such conciseness that all formal elements pale into insignificance. Unhampered by formal preoccupations, the master's impetuous desire for expression is free to develop in its own way.

Form and matter

The formula of Tintoretto's art, which we have attempted to lay down, thus ends in an apparent contradiction; with his pictures he makes us forget that they are painted, or that they are anything else but merely painted. Not in productions of different conception, but in one and the same work, he makes form dissolve into matter and matter into form. This schism is due to the conflict between Tintoretto's personality and his place in history. The High Renaissance had brought art to a pitch which appeared to be perfection; the new period in which he lived had to give new vitality to sentimental matter which had already been used. Mannerism sought to achieve the balance of forces by a rational method which led close to the abysses of mysticism; early Baroque sought to achieve it by augmenting the spiritual element in an enhancement of form. Tintoretto's existence was filled with these contradictions. He was by temperament profoundly anti-intellectual and he was born in an age of rational tendencies; he was the son and heir of the tradition of Venetian painting and destined by fate to consummate the long overdue reconciliation with Central Italian art. His simultaneous exaltation of physical and psychical existence was a presage of the efforts of Baroque art, but owing to the tension which continued to exist between the two he remained in the realm of Mannerism. For Venice he represented the zenith and the close of a golden age of art, for through him an artistic aspiration persisting through several generations, enriched by the achievements of Central Italian art, succeeds once again in bringing forth pure Venetian creations. He had no successors, except his sons and his assistants, who with the faithfulness of vassals defended the citadel of his workshop. His real pupils were those who from time to time caught a breath of his spirit: Caravaggio, Velázquez, Rembrandt, Delacroix. Over and above the vital values which artists of this type found in him, stand the greatness and finality of tradition, the dying notes of which are incorporated in his art. Tintoretto is a modern artist, clothed in the garb of Classic Art.

CHRONOLOGICAL TABLE

1518. At the end of September or the beginning of October Tintoretto was born, according to the entry in the register of deaths of San Marciliano, Venice, where it is stated that he died on May 31st 1594, aged 75 years and eight months. (G. P. Zabeo, Elogio del Tintoretto, Venice 1813.)

1539. Tintoretto lives in the parish of San Cassiano and is described as " mistro Giacomo depentor."

1545. Ceiling-paintings of Apollo and Marsyas (formerly in the Bromley-Davenport collection, London) and Mercury and Argus (lost) for Pietro Aretino.

1546. Fresco in the Arsenal, Belshazzar's Feast (lost).

1547. The Last Supper in San Marcuola.

1548. The Miracle of St. Mark for the Scuola di San Marco, as proved by Aretino's letter to Tintoretto in April of this year (Lettere IV, 181).

1549. Altar-piece in San Marciliano.

1550 ff. Works for the Procuratie.

Ca. 1550. Tintoretto marries Faustina dei Vescovi.

1552. Two pictures of saints for the Magistrato del Sale (later in the Antichie-setta, now in the Accademia).

1552. Four Evangelists for Santa Maria Zobenigo.

1553. Excommunication of Frederick Barbarossa for the Sala del Gran Consiglio in the Ducal Palace (burnt in 1577).

1559. The Pool of Bethesda for the church of San Rocco.

1561. The Marriage at Cana in Santa Maria della Salute.

1562. Tommaso Rangone di Ravenna receives from the Grande Scuola di San Marco, of which he was custodian, permission to have three pictures painted depicting miracles of St. Mark (two are now in the Accademia at Venice and one in the Brera at Milan).

1562. Coronation of Frederick Barbarossa in the Sala del Gran Consiglio in the Ducal Palace (burnt in 1577).

1563. Tintoretto a member of the commission appointed to inspect Zuccati's mosaics for San Marco.

1564. Ceiling-painting in the Albergo di San Rocco and beginning of Tintoretto's permanent connection with the brotherhood.

1565. Crucifixion in the Scuola di San Rocco, of which Tintoretto becomes a member.

1566/67. Tintoretto finishes the decoration of the Albergo and church of San Rocco.

1566. Tintoretto becomes a member of the Florentine Academy.

1566/67. Last Judgement in the Sala dello Scrutinio in the Ducal Palace (destroyed by fire in 1577).

1568. Contract with the Scuola di San Marco for a picture showing the bringing of St. Mark's body to Venice.

1568. First cartoons for the mosaics in San Marco.

1568. Christ in Limbo for San Cassiano.

1571/72. Works for the Libreria.

1572/74. Picture of the Battle of Lepanto for the Ducal Palace (destroyed by fire in 1577).

1574. Tintoretto purchases a house on the Fondamenta dei Mori near the Madonna dell'Orto.

1574. Portrait of King Henri III of France (the original has disappeared; copy in the Ducal Palace).

1575. Beginning of the work on the ceiling of the upper hall of the Scuola di San Rocco.

1576/77. Further work on the ceiling of the upper hall and contract for permanent employment in the Scuola di San Rocco.

1576/81. Paintings in the upper hall of the Scuola di San Rocco.

1577. Temptation of St. Anthony in San Trovaso.

1577. The Ducal Palace damaged by a fire, which destroys a number of Tintoretto's paintings.

1578. Four mythological paintings for the Atrio Quadrato in the Ducal Palace (now in the Anticollegio, in the same palace).

1579/80. Eight scenes from the history of the Gonzagas for Mantua (now in Munich). Journey to Mantua.

1581/84. Votive pictures in the Sala del Collegio at the Ducal Palace.

1583/87. Mural paintings in the ground-floor hall of the Scuola di San Rocco.

1584/87. Painting of the Battle of Zara in the Sala dello Scrutinio at the Ducal Palace.

1585. Tintoretto paints portraits of the Japanese ambassadors who came to Venice on June 7th (lost).

1588. Paradise in the Sala del Gran Consiglio at the Ducal Palace.

1588. Altar-piece in the Scuola di San Rocco.

1590. Death of Marietta Robusti.

1592. Tintoretto is appointed member of the Scuola dei Mercanti and undertakes to paint the Brazen Serpent on the ceiling of the Albergo.

1592/94. Works for San Giorgio Maggiore.

1594. March 30th. Tintoretto makes his will.

1594. May 31st. Death of Tintoretto. He was buried in the family vault of the Vescovi at Madonna dell'Orto.

BIBLIOGRAPHY OF THE PRINCIPAL WORKS
DEALING WITH TINTORETTO

I. Sources

G. Bardi, Dichiarazione di tutte le istorie che si contengono nella Sala dello Scrutino e del Gran Consiglio del Palagio Ducale, 1587.

R. Borghini, Il Riposo della pittura e della scultura, 1584 (Siena edition 1787, III, 116 ff.).

M. Boschini, La Carta del Navigare pittoresco, 1660.

M. Boschini, Le Minere della Pittura Veneziana, 1664.

R. Gallo, La famiglia di Jacopo T., in Ateneo Veneto 1941, pp. 73—92.

A. Guisconi, Tutte le cose notabili ... a Venezia, 1556 (reprinted 1861).

D. Freiherr von Hadeln, Archivarische Beiträge zur Geschichte der venezianischen Kunst, in Italienische Forschungen IV.

G. B. Lorenzi, Monumenti per servire alla Storia del Palazzo Ducale di Venezia, 1868.

Lovisa, Il gran Teatro delle Pitture e Prospettive di Venezia, 1770.

C. Ridolfi, Le Meraviglie dell'Arte, 1648 (new edition by Hadeln, Berlin 1924, II; the Vita of Tintoretto appeared separately in 1642).

F. Sansovino, Venetia Città Nobilissima, 1581.

G. Vasari, Le Vite dei più eccellenti Pittori etc., 1568, G. Milanesi edition, VI, 587 ff.

A. M. Zanetti, Varie Pitture a fresco dei Principali Maestri Veneziani, 1761.

II. Monographs
(arranged according to year of publication)

P. Zabeo, Elogio del T., Venice 1813.

W. Roscoe Osler, T., London 1879.

H. Thode, T., Bielefeld 1901.

I. D. Stoughton Holborn, T., London 1907.

E. M. Phillipps, T., London 1911.

F. P. B. Osmaston, The Art and Genius of T., London 1915.

E. Waldmann, T., Berlin 1921.

E. von der Bercken and A. L. Mayer, T., Munich 1923 (abbreviation: Bercken-Mayer).

Mary Pittaluga, T., Bologna 1925.

F. Fosca, T., Paris 1929.

Viggo Loos, T., motreformationens målare, Norrköping 1940.

L. Coletti, Il T., Bergamo, 1941.

E. von der Bercken, T., Munich 1942.

III. Individual works

B. Berenson, While on T., in Festschrift für M. J. Friedländer, Leipsic, 1927, p. 224.

R. Berliner, Die Tätigkeit T's. in der Schule San Rocco, Kunstchronik, N. F. XXXI, p. 468, 492.

Hadeln, Beiträge zur Tintorettoforschung, Jahrb. d. Preuß. Kunstsamml. XXXII, 13 ff.

Hadeln, Beiträge zur Geschichte des Dogenpalastes, ibid., XXXII, supplement.

Hadeln, Über einige Bildnisse des T., ibid., XLI, p. 32.

Hadeln, Zeichnungen des T., ibid., XLII, p. 82.

Hadeln, Handzeichnungen des T., Berlin 1922.

Hadeln, T. als Cassonemaler, Zeitschr. f. Bild. Kunst, N. F. XXXIII.

Hadeln, Early Works by T., Burlington Magazine XLI, p. 206.

Hadeln, Some Drawings by T., ibid., XLIV, p. 278.

F. P. B. Osmaston, The Paradise of T., London 1910.

R. Pallucchini, T. a San Rocco, 1937.

M. Pittaluga, Criteri Paesistici del T., Arte XXIII, p. 163.

M. Pittaluga, L'Attività del T. in Palazzo Ducale, ibid., XXV, p. 76.

M. Pittaluga, Opere del T. smarrite o di malsicura identificazione, ibid., XXIX., p. 38.

H. Thode, Kritische Studien über T., Repertorium für Kunstwissenschaft XXIII, p. 427; XXIV, p. 7 and 426, XXVII, p. 13 f.

E. Tietze-Conrat, Echte und Unechte T.-Zeichnungen, Graph. Künste, N. F. I, 88.

IV. Varia

B. Berenson, The Venetian Painters of the Renaissance, 1897.

B. Berenson, Italian Pictures of the Renaissance, 1932.

B. Berenson. Pitture Italiane del Rinascimento, 1936.

Max Dvořák, Italienische Kunst II, Munich 1928.

Heinrich Kretschmayr, Geschichte von Venedig III, 1934.

G. Lorenzetti, Venezia e il suo Estuario, 1926.

M. Pevsner, Barockmalerei in den romanischen Ländern, in Handb. der Kunstwissenschaft.

J. Ruskin, Stones of Venice, 1863.

H. Tietze, Tizian, Leben und Werk, 1936.

Hans Tietze and E. Tietze-Conrat, The Drawings of the Venetian Painters of the 15th and 16th Centuries, New York, 1944.

A. Venturi, La Storia dell'Arte Italiana, 9/IV.

L. Venturi, Italian Paintings in America, 1933, III, 544—564.

A NOTE ABOUT THE PLATES

THE ILLUSTRATIONS in this volume, and the catalogue which explains and supplements them, have claims to completeness only in the sense that the Master's essential pictures, in so far as they were accessible, have been reproduced and also those of the doubtful attributions which are more important and are recognized by reliable authorities or at least mentioned. For paintings still in the art market it seemed advisable to use especially severe reserve. Of the drawings we have included only a few characteristic examples.

The essential conditions for the inclusion of a picture in this volume have been the conviction that it is a work by the master's own hand or the power of original conception it reveals. With a painter like Tintoretto, who from his early days had an atelier of which he made more and more use as time went on, there is bound to be a conflict of opinion as to which of these two characteristics—each of which may coincide with a lack of the other—is to be taken as authoritative in each individual case. There is no absolute formula for solving this conflict, but only a scientific standard which endeavours to measure every production by the inner conception elaborated by a school of artists. This conception is based mainly on those works which have always been supported by a reliable tradition. That in the case of Tintoretto far more works are still in their original locations in Venice than in the case of Titian fills the spiritual picture which they produce with organic strength and unity. Though there are obscure places in this picture—Tintoretto's youthful development, the practice of his atelier, his production of portraits, which seems to have been based on broad business lines—nevertheless his artistic personality is more clearly circumscribed in its essential features than that of many other important painters. Judged by what we know for certain, much that has been attributed to Tintoretto since the attention of art-lovers has been drawn to him must be rejected. A connoisseurship which considered it a sufficient argument for attributing a work to Tintoretto if certain features of the work in question were reminiscent of him, instead of requiring the inner certainty that in every respect it tallied with his artistic essence and rank, has collected a sorry assembly of doubtful productions round the bright nucleus of his work. It is characteristic that this excessive multiplication consists to a considerable extent of portraits, a field in which there has been hitherto hardly an attempt at critical arrangement and methodical sifting. To accept such attributions, which are based on arbitrary assumptions—sometimes, it is true, intuitive and felicitous—in a popular monograph, would be, in my opinion, a breach of the first duty incumbent upon the author of such a work, which is to offer what is reliable to the larger circles of the public outside the inner ring of experts. It should therefore be understood that among the pictures omitted from this volume there are some which I think might be by Tintoretto; they are discussible, but there is no need to discuss them in a volume like the present. On the other hand, a few are included about whose autograph character I feel less certain to-day after the long interruption in the preparation of the book. For technical reasons they cannot be eliminated now. In the notes of the catalogue I have expressed my present opinion in such cases.

H. T.

THE PLATES

1. SELF-PORTRAIT (?). About 1548. London, Victoria & Albert Museum. ⟨18¹/₈ × 14³/₈⟩

2. THE WOMAN TAKEN IN ADULTERY. 1542–1545. Dresden, Staatsgalerie. ⟨74¹/₂ x 140⟩

3. THE CONTEST BETWEEN APOLLO AND MARSYAS. 1545. London, formerly in the Bromley-Davenport collection. ⟨54 × 93⟩

4. THE NATIVITY OF JOHN THE BAPTIST. Early period. Venice, San Zaccaria. ⟨106¼ x 80¼⟩

5. THE VISITATION. Early period. Bologna, Pinacoteca. ⟨98³/₈ × 57¹/₂⟩

6. VENUS, VULCAN AND CUPID. Early period. Florence, Palazzo Pitti.

7. THE RAISING OF LAZARUS. About 1548. Leipzig, Städtisches Museum der Bildenden Künste. ⟨70 × 99¹/₄⟩

9. THE MIRACLE OF THE LOAVES AND FISHES. 1544—1547. New York, Metropolitan Museum. ⟨61¼ x 161⅛⟩

11. ST. URSULA AND HER VIRGINS. About 1545. Venice, San Lazzaro dei Mendicanti. ⟨130 × 70⟩

13. GROUP OF APOSTLES. Detail from the Last Supper ⟨Fig. 20⟩

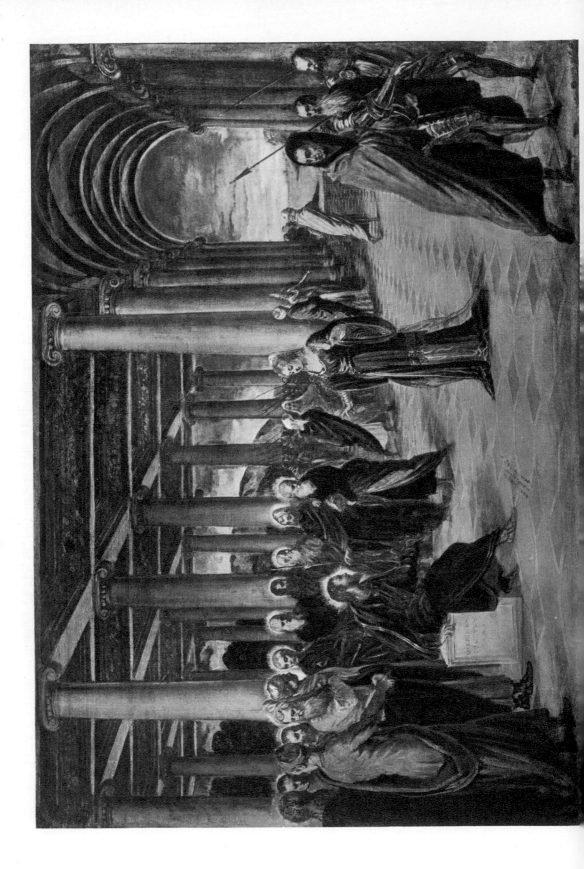

15. THE WOMAN TAKEN IN ADULTERY. Early period. Amsterdam, vom Rath collection.

16. THE WASHING OF FEET. About 1545. Salisbury, Wilton House. ⟨57⅞ x 99⅝⟩

17. THE WASHING OF FEET. About 1545. Escorial.

2

18. PORTRAIT OF A NOBLEMAN. 1545. Hampton Court. ⟨41³/₄ × 34¹/₂⟩

19. PORTRAIT OF NICOLÒ PRIULI. 1545—1549. Venice, Cà d'Oro. ⟨49¹/₄ x 41¹/₄⟩

20. THE LAST SUPPER. 1547. Venice, San Marcuola. ⟨61³/₄ x 174¹/₂⟩

21. ST. MARK RESCUING A SLAVE. 1548. Venice, Accademia. ⟨163¹/₂ x 214⟩

22. DETAIL FROM THE MIRACLE OF ST. MARK (Fig. 21)

23. GROUP OF FIGURES. Detail from the Miracle of St. Agnes ⟨Fig. 27⟩

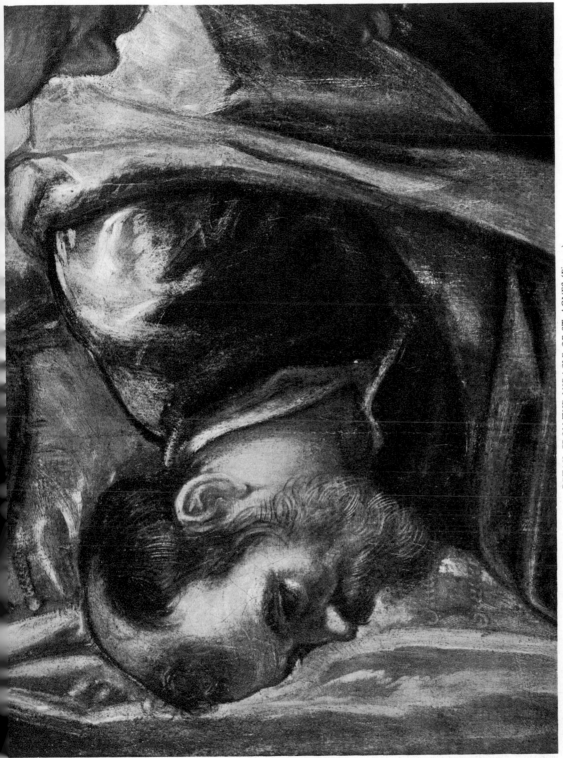

26. ST. MARCELLIANO. 1549. Venice, San Marziale. ⟨148×71¼⟩

27. THE MIRACLE OF ST. AGNES. About 1550. Venice, Madonna dell'Orto. ⟨157¹/₂ × 78³/₄⟩

29. GOD THE FATHER WITH ADAM AND EVE AT THE TREE OF KNOWLEDGE. 1550–1551. Florence, Uffizi. (58¼ x 46½)

31. CAIN AND ABEL. About 1550—1551. Venice, Accademia. (55 × 81½)

32. BELSHAZZAR'S FEAST. About 1545. Vienna, Gemäldegalerie. ⟨11³/₈ x 61⟩

33. THE QUEEN OF SHEBA BEFORE SOLOMON. About 1545. Vienna, Gemäldegalerie. ⟨11³/₈ x 61³/₄⟩

35. THE VENGEANCE OF SAMSON. About 1548. Vienna, Gemäldegalerie. ⟨11³/₈ × 61⟩

36. THE PROMISE TO DAVID. About 1548. Vienna, Gemäldegalerie. ⟨11³/₈ × 61⟩

37. DAVID BRINGING BACK THE ARK OF THE COVENANT. About 1548. Vienna, Gemäldegalerie. ⟨11³/₈ × 61³/₄⟩

38. TWO MEN. Detail from the Prostration of Bathsheba (Fig. 34)

39. TWO CROWNED FIGURES. Detail from the Promise to David ⟨Fig. 36⟩

40. THE QUEEN OF SHEBA BEFORE SOLOMON. Early work. Aachen, Städtisches Suermondt-Museum. ⟨10¹/₄ x 17³/₄⟩

42. MEN IN LANDSCAPE. Detail from David bringing back the Ark of the Covenant ⟨Fig. 37⟩

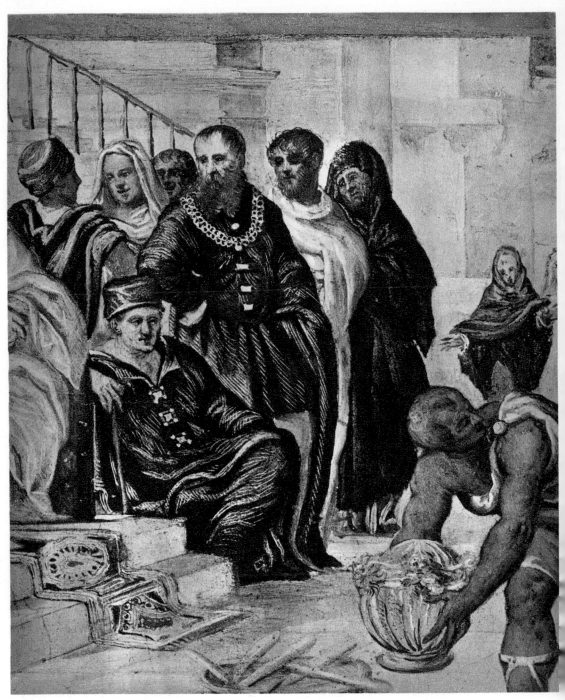

43. GROUP OF FIGURES. Detail from the Queen of Sheba before Solomon ⟨Fig. 33⟩

44. A SERVANT. Detail from the Feast of Belshazzar ⟨Fig. 32⟩

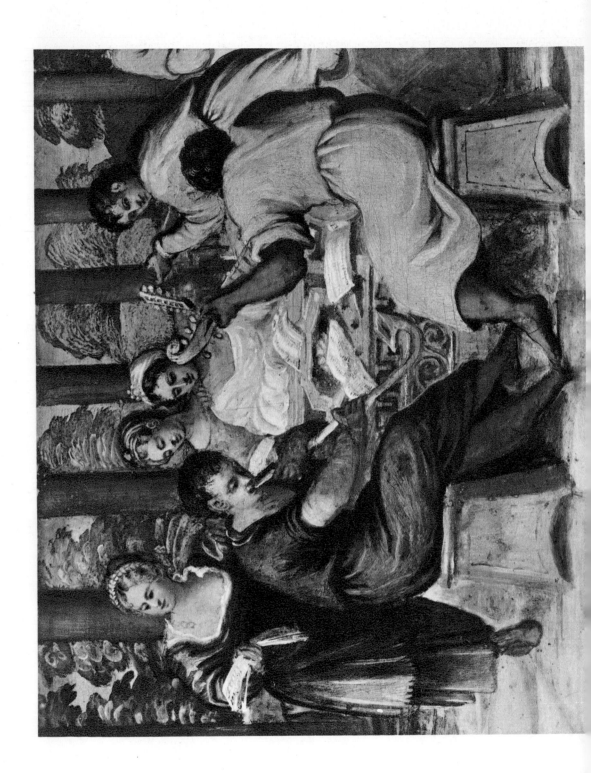

46. GROUP OF FIGURES. Detail from the Promise to David ⟨Fig. 36⟩

50. THE CRUCIFIXION. 1555–1560. Venice, Santa Maria del Rosario. ⟨117 × 65⟩

49. ST. LOUIS, ST. JEROME AND ST. ANDREW. 1557 or earlier. Venice, Accademia. ⟨72¹/₂ × 52³/₈⟩

51. THE EVANGELISTS JOHN AND MARK. 1552. Venice, Santa Maria Zobenigo. ⟨101 × 59⟩

52. THE EVANGELISTS LUKE AND MATTHEW. 1552. Venice, Santa Maria Zobenigo. ⟨102 × 59⟩

53. **ST. JOHN THE EVANGELIST.** Detail from Fig. 51.

54. HEAD OF ST. MATTHEW. Detail from Fig. 52.

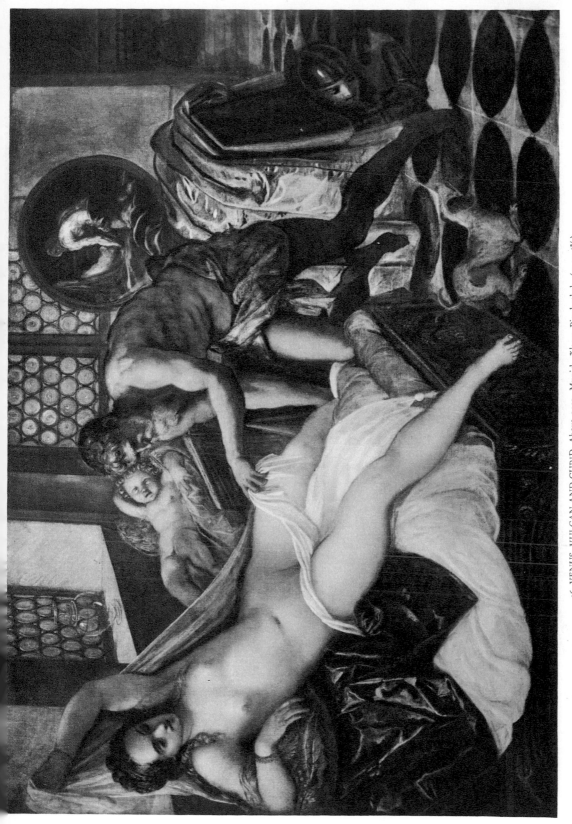

56. VENUS, VULCAN AND CUPID. About 1550. Munich, Ältere Pinakothek. (52 x 76⅜)

58. JUDITH AND HOLOFERNES. 1550—1560. Madrid, Prado. (74 x 98¾)

60. DANAE. 1555–1560. Lyons, Museum. ⟨60¼ x 77½⟩

61. DETAIL FROM SUSANNA BATHING ⟨cf. the colour plate⟩

62. DETAIL FROM SUSANNA BATHING ⟨cf. the colour plate⟩

64. THE RESCUE OF ARSINOE. 1555–1560. Dresden, Staatsgalerie. ⟨60¹/₄ x 98³/₄⟩

65. SKETCH FOR THE CORPSE IN ST. GEORGE AND THE DRAGON ⟨cf. the colour plate⟩. Paris, Louvre.

66. THE PRINCESS. Detail from St. George and the Dragon (cf. the colour plate)

68. LANDSCAPE. Detail from St. George and the Dragon ⟨cf. the colour plate⟩

70. THE TIBURTINE SIBYL AND AUGUSTUS. About 1550—1555. Formerly Venice, Sant'Anna. (Present location unknown)

72. THE POOL OF BETHESDA. 1559. Venice, San Rocco. ⟨93³/4 x 220¹/2⟩

73. SKETCH FOR THE RETURN OF THE PRODIGAL SON ⟨Fig. 74⟩. Florence, Uffizi. ⟨14⁷/₈ × 10⁸/₆⟩

74. THE PARABLE OF THE PRODIGAL SON. About 1560. Venice, Ducal Palace, Sala degli Inquisitori. ⟨80 x 80⟩

75. PORTRAIT OF A GENTLEMAN WITH A GOLD CHAIN. About 1550. Madrid, Prado. ⟨40½ × 30⟩

76. PORTRAIT OF A MAN. 1553. Vienna, Gemäldegalerie. ⟨45¼ x 38⟩

77. PORTRAIT OF ANDREA CAPPELLO. 1555—1560. Venice, Accademia. ⟨44⁷/₈ × 35⟩

78. PORTRAIT OF DOGE FRANCESCO DONATO. 1547—1553. Bremen, Kunsthalle. ⟨27¹/₈ x 23¹/₂⟩

79. PORTRAIT OF A LADY IN MOURNING. Early period. Dresden, Staatsgalerie. ⟨41 × 34¹/₁⟩

80. PORTRAIT OF A NOBLEMAN. 1555. Dublin, National Gallery of Ireland. ⟨45¼ x 31½⟩

81. PORTRAIT OF A MAN. About 1560. Berlin, Kaiser-Friedrich-Museum. ⟨23¼ × 17¾⟩

82. PORTRAIT OF JACOPO SORANZO. About 1551. Milan, Castello Sforzesco. ⟨29¹/₂ x 23⁵/₈⟩

83. THE VIRGIN WITH THE CHILD AND FOUR SENATORS. Venice, Accademia. ⟨74 × 57⟩

84. PORTRAIT OF A YOUTH WITH A BOOK. About 1560. Amsterdam, Goudstikker Collection. ⟨37¼ × 29½⟩

85. SPECTATORS. Detail from the Invention of the Cross ⟨Fig. 87⟩

86. GROUP OF FIGURES FROM THE INVENTION OF THE CROSS ⟨Fig. 87⟩

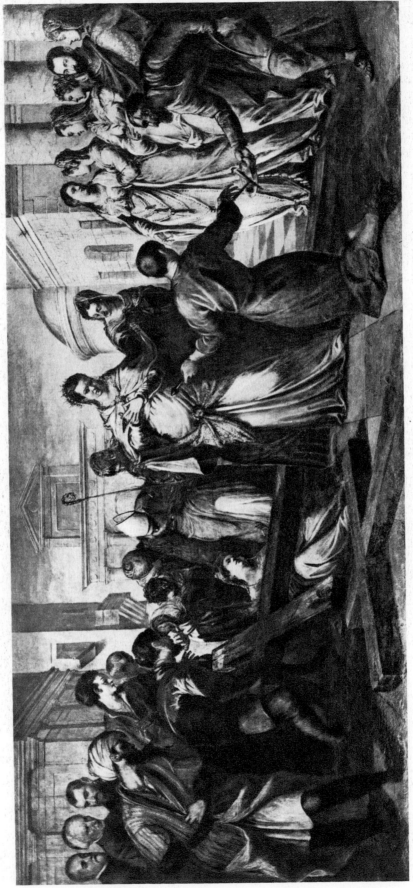

87. THE INVENTION OF THE CROSS. About 1560. Venice, Santa Maria Mater Domini. (89¾ x 200)

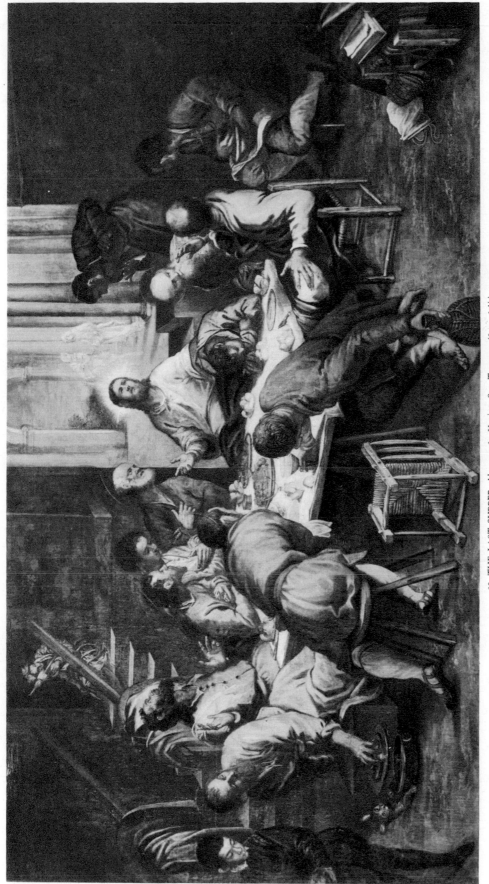

88. THE LAST SUPPER. About 1560. Venice, San Trovaso. ⟨87 x 162½⟩

6

89. ST. HELENA WITH OTHER SAINTS. 1560—1570. Milan, Brera. ⟨108¼ × 65⟩

90. ALLEGORY WITH DOGE GIROLAMO PRIULI. About 1560. Venice, Ducal Palace.

91. THE LAST JUDGEMENT (lower portion). About 1560. Venice, Madonna dell'Orto.

92. THE GOLDEN CALF (lower portion). About 1560. Venice, Madonna dell'Orto.

93 b. THE GOLDEN CALF ⟨upper portion, cf. Fig. 92⟩.

93 a. THE LAST JUDGEMENT ⟨upper portion, cf. Fig. 91⟩.

94. THE GOLDEN CALF. Detail from Fig. 92

95. THE VISION OF ST. PETER. About 1560. Venice, Madonna dell'Orto.

96. MARTYRDOM OF ST. CHRISTOPHER. About 1560. Venice, Madonna dell'Orto.

98. THE PRESENTATION OF THE VIRGIN. About 1552. Venice, Madonna dell'Orto. ⟨169 × 189⟩

99. MOTHER AND CHILD. Detail from the Presentation of the Virgin ⟨Fig. 98⟩

100. WOMAN AND CHILD. Detail from the Presentation of the Virgin (Fig. 98)

101. JUDITH AND HOLOFERNES. About 1560. Madrid, Prado. ⟨27⁷/₈ × 46¹/₂⟩

102. THE CHASTE SUSANNA. About 1560. Madrid, Prado. ⟨27⅛ x 45¾⟩

103. JOSEPH AND POTIPHAR'S WIFE. 1563—1570. Madrid, Prado. ⟨21 1/4 × 46⟩

104. THE FINDING OF MOSES. 1550—1560. Madrid, Prado. (22 × 46¹/₂)

105. THE QUEEN OF SHEBA BEFORE SOLOMON. About 1560. Madrid, Prado. ⟨22³/₄ × 8¹/₈⟩

107 THE NINE MUSES. Hampton Court. ⟨83½ x 119¾⟩

108. ONE OF THE MUSES, PLAYING THE VIOLA. Amsterdam, Otto Lanz Collection. ⟨50 × 32¹/₄⟩

109. CHRIST IN THE HOUSE OF THE PHARISEE. 1562. Padua, Museo Civico.

110. ROUGH SEA. Detail from St. Mark rescuing the Saracen (Fig. 111)

111. ST. MARK RESCUING THE SARACEN. About 1562. Venice, Accademia. ⟨166 × 124¹/₂⟩

112. THE FINDING OF THE BODY OF ST. MARK. About 1562. Milan, Brera. ⟨159¹/₂ × 159¹/₂⟩

113. THE REMOVAL OF THE BODY OF ST. MARK. About 1562. Venice, Accademia. (166 x 124½)

114. APOSTLE. Detail from the Last Supper ⟨Fig. 88⟩

115. SPECTATOR. Detail from the Last Supper ⟨Fig. 140⟩

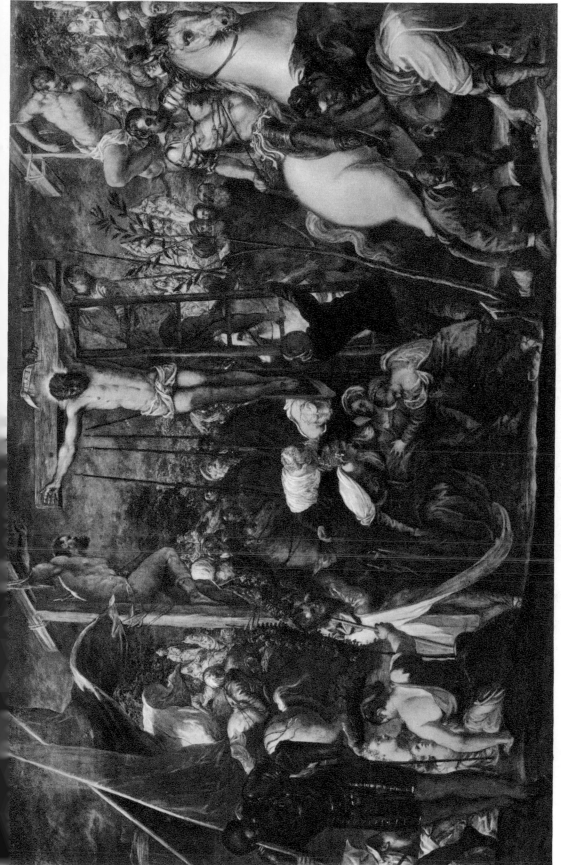

117. THE CRUCIFIXION. 1560—1565. Venice, Accademia. ⟨110/4 x 96⟩

119. PIETA. 1563—1571. Milan, Brera. (42½ x 67)

120. ALLEGORICAL FIGURE. About 1565. Venice, Scuola di San Rocco, Sala dell'Albergo.

121. ALLEGORICAL FIGURE. About 1565. Venice, Scuola di San Rocco, Sala dell'Albergo.

122. ST. ROCH IN GLORY. 1564. Venice, Scuola di San Rocco, Sala dell'Albergo.

123. CHRIST BEFORE PILATE. 1566. Venice, Scuola di San Rocco, Sala dell'Albergo. ⟨217 x 159½⟩

124. CHRIST BEARING THE CROSS. 1566. Venice, Scuola di San Rocco, Sala dell'Albergo. ⟨205½ x 159½⟩

126. CHRIST BEARING THE CROSS. Detail from Fig. 124.

127. ST. JOHN. Detail from the Crucifixion (cf. folding plate)

128. HOLY WOMEN. Detail from the Crucifixion (cf. folding plate)

129. MAN DIGGING. Detail from the Crucifixion (cf. folding plate)

130. CHRIST ON THE CROSS. Detail from the Crucifixion (cf. folding plate)

131. HEAD OF A MAN. Detail from the Crucifixion ⟨cf. folding plate⟩

132. HEAD OF A MAN. Detail from the Crucifixion ⟨cf. folding plate⟩

133. STUDY FOR A FIGURE ON HORSEBACK IN THE CRUCIFIXION. Drawing. London, Victoria & Albert Museum.
⟨12¹/₄ × 8⁵/₈⟩

134. MAN PULLING ROPE. Detail from the Crucifixion ⟨cf. folding plate⟩

135. ST. ROCH MINISTERING TO SUFFERERS FROM THE PLAGUE. Venice, San Rocco. (118 x 265)

136. ST. ROCH IN PRISON. 1567. Venice, San Rocco. (118 x 264½)

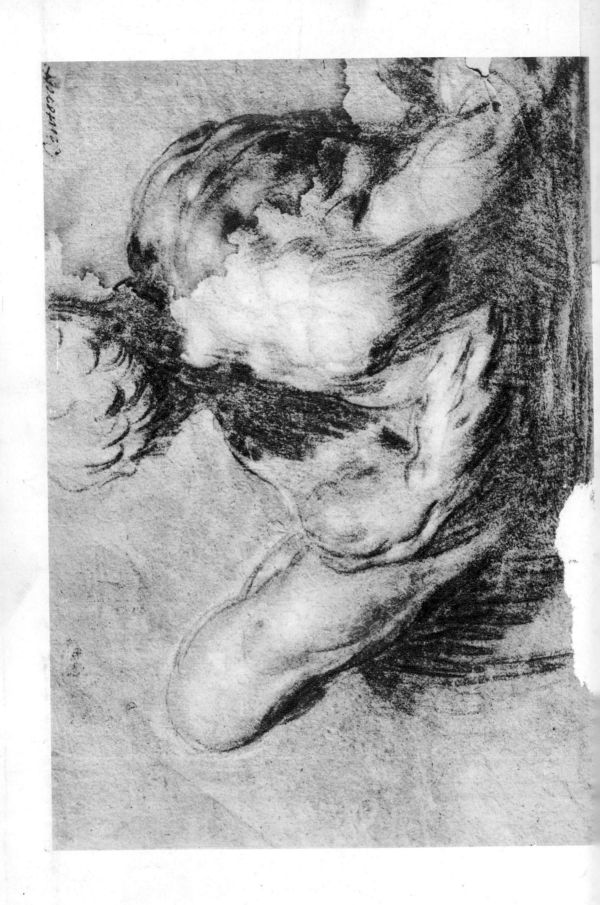

138. ANGEL. Detail from St. Roch in Prison ⟨Fig. 136⟩

9

139. THE WASHING OF FEET. 1560–1565. London, National Gallery. ⟨80 × 160⟩

140. THE LAST SUPPER. 1565—1570. Venice, San Paolo. ⟨89³/₄ × 210¹/₂⟩

141. THE ENTOMBMENT. 1560—1570. London, Bridgewater House. ⟨77 × 57½⟩

142. THE DEPOSITION. About 1560—1565. Caen, Museum

144. THE CRUCIFIXION. 1568. Venice, San Cassiano. ⟨134½ x 146⟩

145. MARY AND JOHN. Detail from the Crucifixion ⟨Fig. 144⟩

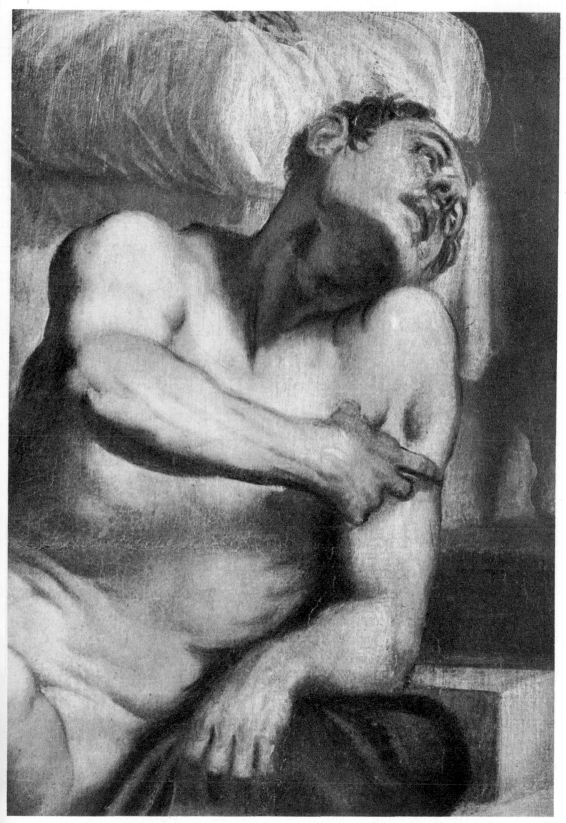

146. SICK MAN. Detail from St. Roch ministering to Sufferers from the Plague ⟨Fig. 135⟩

147. ANGEL. Detail from Christ in Limbo ⟨Fig. 143⟩

148. THE ORIGIN OF THE MILKY WAY. After 1570. London, National Gallery. ⟨58 x 65¹/₂⟩

149. THE VIRGIN WITH THE CHILD, SEVERAL SAINTS AND THREE CHAMBERLAINS. 1566. Venice. Accademia. ⟨87³/4 x 205⟩

150. GROUP-PORTRAIT OF THE PELLEGRINI FAMILY. London, R. Smith-Barry Collection. ⟨79 × 178⟩

151. PORTRAIT OF ALVISE CORNARO. About 1565. Florence, Palazzo Pitti. ⟨44 × 33½⟩

JO.PAVLVS. CORNELIVS
HERMOLAI A . Æ SVÆ
XXXII A CHR MDLXI.

152. PORTRAIT OF PAOLO CORNARO DELLE ANTICAGLIE. 1561. Ghent, Gallery.

153. PORTRAIT OF AN OLD MAN WITH A BOY. About 1565—1570. Vienna, Gemäldegalerie. ⟨40 × 32³/₄⟩

CHRIST IN THE HOUSE OF MARY AND MARTHA. Munich, Ältere Pinakothek. ⟨77½ × 51⟩

154. PORTRAIT OF DOGE PIETRO LOREDAN. 1567—1570. New York, John R. Delafield collection.

155. PORTRAIT OF JACOPO SANSOVINO. 1566. Florence, Uffizi. ⟨27¹/₂ × 25¹/₂⟩

PENSATE LA FIN

1569

156. ST. MARK WITH THREE PROCURATORS OF VENICE. About 1571. Berlin, Kaiser-Friedrich-Museum. ⟨82 × 69¹/₂⟩

157. PORTRAIT OF A VENETIAN ADMIRAL About 1570. Florence, Uffizi. ⟨50 × 39⟩

158. PORTRAIT OF DOGE ALVISE MOCENIGO. 1570—1577. Venice, Accademia. ⟨45¹/₈ × 37¹/₂⟩

159. STUDY FOR A PHILOSOPHER IN THE LIBRERIA. 1570—1571. Florence, Uffizi. ⟨11³/₄ × 8⟩

160. A PHILOSOPHER. 1571—1572. Venice, Libreria. ⟨92 × 54⟩

161. A PHILOSOPHER. 1571—1572. Venice, Libreria. (92 × 54)

162. A PHILOSOPHER. 1571—1572. Venice, Libreria. ⟨92 × 54⟩

163. A PHILOSOPHER. 1571—1572. Venice, Libreria. (92 × 54)

164. HEAD OF A PHILOSOPHER. Detail from Fig. 163.

165. THE RAISING OF LAZARUS. 1576. Lübeck, Katharinenmuseum. ⟨125¹/₄ x 100¹/₂⟩

166. THE DREAMS OF MEN. Detroit, Institute of Arts. ⟨145 x 84¼⟩

167. THE ANNUNCIATION. 1574—1584. Venice, San Rocco.

168. THE VIRGIN WITH THE CHILD AND SAINTS MARK AND LUKE. About 1570—1580. Berlin, Kaiser-Friedrich-Museum.
(89³/₄ x 63)

170. THE ANNUNCIATION. About 1570—1580. Berlin, Kaiser-Friedrich-Museum. ⟨79 × 113¹/₂⟩

172. THE TRINITY. About 1570—1575. Turin, Gallery. (48 x 71¼)

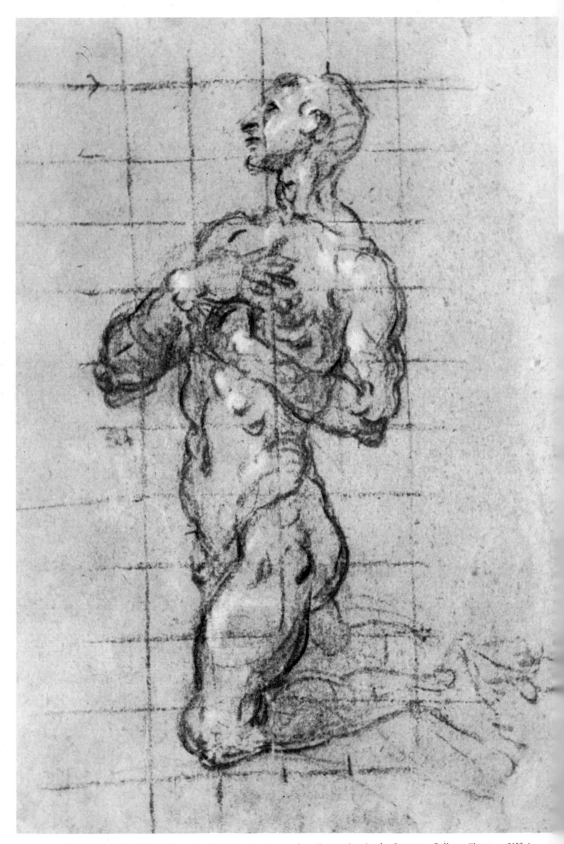

173. STUDY IN THE NUDE. Drawing. Used for the Immaculate Conception in the Stuttgart Gallery. Florence, Uffizi.
⟨13³/₈ × 9³/₈⟩

174. ST. JUSTINA WITH THREE TREASURERS. 1580. Venice, Accademia. ⟨85 x 71¼⟩

175. THE VIRGIN WITH SAINTS COSMAS AND DAMIAN. 1570—1580. Venice, Accademia. ⟨134 × 98¹/₂⟩

176. THE TEMPTATION OF ST. ANTHONY. 1577. Venice, San Trovaso. ⟨111 × 65⟩

178. THE LAST SUPPER. About 1580. Venice, San Stefano. ⟨137½ x 208½⟩

179. SO-CALLED SELF-PORTRAIT. 1573. Venice, Scuola di San Rocco. ⟨28¼ x 22½⟩

180. PORTRAIT OF A VENETIAN SENATOR. 1570—1580. Richmond, Collection of Sir Herbert Cook, Bart. ⟨31¹/₂ x 23⁵/₈⟩

181. SO-CALLED PORTRAIT OF SEBASTIANO VENIER. About 1580. Madrid, Prado. ⟨32¼ x 26⅜⟩

180. PORTRAIT OF A VENETIAN SENATOR. 1570—1580. Richmond, Collection of Sir Herbert Cook, Bart. ⟨31¹/₂ × 23⁵/₈⟩

181. SO-CALLED PORTRAIT OF SEBASTIANO VENIER. About 1580. Madrid, Prado. ⟨32¹/₄ × 26³/₈⟩

182. PORTRAIT OF A VENETIAN SENATOR. 1570—1580. Madrid, Prado. ⟨30¹/₄ x 24³/₄⟩

183. PORTRAIT OF A VENETIAN SENATOR. Late period. Rochester, N.Y., George Eastman Collection. ⟨43¹/₄ × 34¹/₂⟩

184. PORTRAIT OF THE PROCURATOR NICOLO PRIULI. Late period. New York, Frick Collection. ⟨43¼ × 34½⟩

185. PORTRAIT OF VINCENZO MOROSINI. 1578—1588. London, National Gallery. ⟨33⁷/₈ × 20⁷/₈⟩

186. THE BRAZEN SERPENT. 1575—1576. Venice, Scuola di San Rocco. ⟨330 x 206⟩

187. MOSES BRINGING FORTH WATER FROM THE ROCK. 1577. Venice, Scuola di San Rocco. ⟨179 × 206⟩

188. THE GATHERING OF THE MANNA. 1577. Venice, Scuola di San Rocco. ⟨179 × 206⟩

189 and 190. THE VISION OF MOSES—ELIJAH FED BY THE ANGEL. About 1580. Venice, Scuola di San Rocco. ⟨147 × 104⟩

191. THE PILLAR OF FIRE IN THE WILDERNESS.
Venice, Scuola di San Rocco. ⟨147 × 104⟩

192. ELISHA MULTIPLYING THE LOAVES.
Venice, Scuola di San Rocco. ⟨147 × 104⟩

193. THE SACRIFICE OF ISAAC. About 1580. Venice, Scuola di San Rocco. ⟨147 × 104⟩

194. JACOB'S LADDER.
Venice, Scuola di San Rocco. ⟨260 × 104⟩

195. THE VISION OF EZEKIEL.
About 1578. Venice, Scuola di San Rocco. ⟨260 × 143⟩

196. THE SALVATION OF JONAH. About 1578. Venice, Scuola di San Rocco. ⟨104 × 147⟩

197 and 198. ADAM AND EVE.—THE PASCHAL FEAST. About 1578. Venice, Scuola di San Rocco ⟨104 × 147⟩

199. THE VISION OF ST. ROCH. 1588. Venice, Scuola di San Rocco. ⟨195 × 97⟩

200. THE NATIVITY. 1576—1581. Venice, Scuola di San Rocco. ⟨213 × 173⟩

201. THE TEMPTATION OF CHRIST. 1576—1581. Venice, Scuola di San Rocco. ⟨212 × 130⟩

202. THE RESURRECTION. 1576—1581. Venice, Scuola di San Rocco. ⟨208 × 191⟩

203. THE ASCENSION. 1576—1581. Venice, Scuola di San Rocco. ⟨212 × 128⟩

204. THE BAPTISM OF CHRIST. 1576—1581. Venice, Scuola di San Rocco. ⟨212 × 183⟩

205. THE POOL OF BETHESDA. 1576—1581. Venice, Scuola di San Rocco. ⟨210×208⟩

206. THE AGONY IN THE GARDEN. 1576—1581. Venice, Scuola di San Rocco. ⟨210×181⟩

207. THE RAISING OF LAZARUS. 1576—1581. Venice, Scuola di San Rocco. ⟨213 × 140⟩

208. THE LAST SUPPER. 1576—1581. Venice, Scuola di San Rocco. ⟨212 x 192⟩

209. THE MIRACLE OF THE LOAVES AND FISHES. 1576—1581. Venice, Scuola di San Rocco. ⟨206 x 187⟩

282. DRESSER. Detail from the Last Supper (Fig. 208)

213. STUDY AFTER A SCULPTURE. Drawing. Berlin, Kupferstichkabinett ⟨16½ x 11⟩

214. SATAN. Detail from the Temptation of Christ (Fig. 201)

215. **CHRIST.** Detail from the Temptation of Christ ⟨Fig. 201⟩

216. HEAD OF A DONOR. Detail from the Baptism of Christ (Fig. 204)

217. TWO APOSTLES. Detail from the Ascension ⟨Fig. 203⟩

218. HEAD OF A SHEPHERD. Detail from the Nativity ⟨Fig. 200⟩

220. THE BATTLE ON THE TARO. About 1579. Munich, Ältere Pinakothek. ⟨106³/₄ × 170¹/₂⟩

290 THE INVESTITURE OF G. F. GONZAGA WITH THE DUKEDOM OF MANTUA. About 1579. Munich, Ältere Pinakothek. (87³/₄ x 170)

222. THE BATTLE ON THE ADIGE. About 1579. Munich, Ältere Pinakothek. (107½ x 152)

224. THE CAPTURE OF PARMA. 1580. Munich, Ältere Pinakothek. ⟨83⅓ x 108½⟩

226. VULCAN AND THE CYCLOPES. 1578. Venice, Ducal Palace. Sala dell'Anticollegio. ⟨57 x 61½⟩

228. BACCHUS AND ARIADNE. 1578. Venice, Ducal Palace, Sala dell'Anticollegio. ⟨57·¹/₂ × 61·³/₄⟩

229. VENICE AS QUEEN OF THE SEAS. 1581—1584. Venice, Ducal Palace, Sala del Senato.

230. HEAD OF BACCHUS. Detail from Bacchus and Ariadne ⟨Fig. 228⟩

232. VOTIVE PICTURE OF DOGE FRANCESCO DONATO. 1581—1584. Venice, Ducal Palace, Sala del Collegio.

233. VOTIVE PICTURE OF DOGE ALVISE MOCENIGO. 1581—1584. Venice, Ducal Palace, Sala del Collegio.

234. DOGE ALVISE MOCENIGO PRAYING BEFORE CHRIST. 1577—1581. New York, Metropolitan Museum. ⟨38⁵/₈ x 78¹/₄⟩

236. THE CAPTURE OF ZARA. 1584—1587. Venice, Ducal Palace, Sala dello Scrutinio.

237 and 238. THE DEFENCE OF BRESCIA. — THE VICTORY ON THE LAKE OF GARDA. 1580—1584.
Venice, Ducal Palace, Sala del Gran Consiglio.

239. STUDY IN THE NUDE FOR A BOWMAN IN THE CAPTURE OF ZARA ⟨Fig. 236⟩. Drawing.
Florence, Uffizi. ⟨14⁹/₈ × 8⁵/₈⟩

240. THE VENETIAN AMBASSADORS BEFORE FREDERICK BARBAROSSA. 1584—1587. Venice, Ducal Palace,
Sala del Gran Consiglio.

241. CHRIST, THE VIRGIN AND SAINTS. Detail from the Paradise ⟨cf. folding plate⟩

242. POOR SOULS. Detail from the sketch for the Paradise ⟨Fig. 244⟩

243. THE FLAGELLATION. Late period. Vienna, Gemäldegalerie. ⟨46¹/₂ × 41³/₄⟩

244. PARADISE. About 1579. Paris, Louvre. ⟨64¹/₈ x 142¹/₂⟩

245. NAVAL BATTLE ("Rape of Helena"). Late period. Madrid, Prado. ⟨73¼ x 121⟩

247. THE FLIGHT INTO EGYPT. 1583–1587. Venice, Scuola di San Rocco. ⟨165 × 228½⟩

THE ADORATION OF THE MAGI. 1582–1587. Venice, Scuola di San Rocco. (167 × 215¹/₂)

249. THE PRESENTATION IN THE TEMPLE. Venice, Scuola di San Rocco. ⟨173 × 190⟩

251. FOLLOWERS ON HORSEBACK. Detail from the Adoration of the Magi ⟨Fig. 248⟩

252. THE HOLY FAMILY. Detail from the Flight into Egypt ⟨Fig. 247⟩

253. WOMAN AND CHILD. Detail from the Massacre of the Innocents ⟨Fig. 258⟩

254. HEAD OF THE VIRGIN. Detail from the Adoration of the Magi ⟨Fig. 248⟩

255. HEAD OF THE VIRGIN. Detail from the Annunciation ⟨Fig. 246⟩

256. WOMAN'S HEAD. Detail from the Massacre of the Innocents ⟨Fig. 258⟩

257. HEADS OF MARY AND ELISABETH. Detail from the Visitation ⟨Fig. 263⟩

259. THE ASSUMPTION. Venice, Scuola di San Rocco. ⟨167 x 231⟩

RESTI ANTONIVS FLORIAN ANNO. MDCCLXXXIV.

260. ST. MARY AEGYPTIACA. 1583—1587. Venice, Scuola di San Rocco. ⟨167 × 83⟩

261. ST. MARY MAGDALEN. 1583—1587. Venice, Scuola di San Rocco. ⟨167 × 82⟩

263. THE VISITATION. About 1585. Venice, Scuola di San Rocco. ⟨63 × 94½⟩

264. MULE-DRIVER. Detail from the Gathering of the Manna ⟨Fig. 274⟩

265. JUDAS AND THE INFORMERS. Detail from the Agony in the Garden ⟨Fig. 266⟩

266. THE AGONY IN THE GARDEN. About 1580. Venice, Santo Stefano. ⟨131¹/₂ × 115¹/₄⟩

267. THE WASHING OF FEET. About 1580. Venice, Santo Stefano.

268. BATTLE BETWEEN ST. MICHAEL AND SATAN. Late period. Dresden, Staatsgalerie. ⟨125¼ × 86½⟩

269. ST. MICHAEL WITH A DONOR. Late period. Venice, San Giuseppe di Castello.

270. THE BAPTISM OF CHRIST. 1580—1585. Venice, San Silvestro. ⟨111¹/₂ × 67³/₄⟩

271. " PAX TIBI, MARCE ". Late period. Venice, Accademia. ⟨153¹/₂ × 126³/₄⟩

273. GROUP OF FIGURES. Detail from the Gathering of the Manna ⟨Fig. 274⟩

275. THE LAST SUPPER. 1592—1594. Venice, San Giorgio Maggiore. ⟨144 X 224⟩

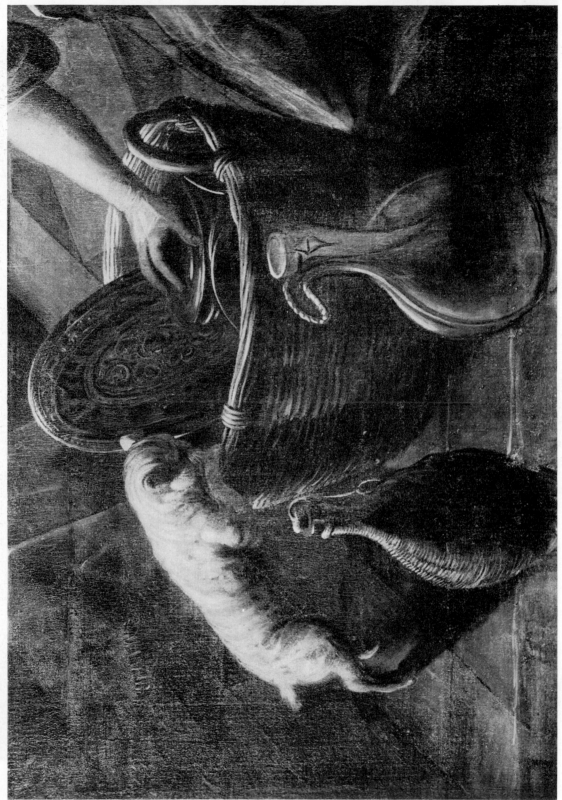

275. STILL-LIFE. Detail from the Last Supper ⟨Fig. 275⟩

279. MARTYRDOM OF SAINTS COSMAS AND DAMIAN.

278. MARTYRDOM OF ST. STEPHEN.

280. ST. CATHERINE ON THE WHEEL. Late period. Venice, Santa Caterina. ⟨63 × 89⟩

281. ADORATION OF THE MAGI. Late period. Venice, San Trovaso.

282. THE EXPULSION OF JOACHIM FROM THE TEMPLE. Studio work. Late period. Venice, San Trovaso.

283. THE ENTOMBMENT. 1594. Venice, San Giorgio Maggiore. ⟨113³/₈ × 65³/₈⟩

APPENDIX

284. PORTRAIT OF A MAN. About 1570. Sands Point, L. I., L. M. Rabinowitz Collection. ⟨48³/₄ × 37¹/₄⟩

285. TARQUIN AND LUCRECE. About 1556—59. New York, Richard Goetz Collection

286. THE CAPTURE OF ST. ROCH AT THE BATTLE OF MONTPELLIER. London, Messrs. Colnaghi. ⟨38³/₄×79⟩

287. FINDING OF MOSES. 1550—60. New York, Metropolitan Museum. (30¹/₂ x 52³/₄)

288. THE WORSHIP OF THE GOLDEN CALF. Washington, D. C., National Gallery of Art. ⟨62⁵/₈ × 107⟩

289. POET IN LANDSCAPE. Princeton, N. J., Museum of Historic Art. ⟨23¹/₂ x 18⟩

THE CATALOGUE

Plates refer to illustrations in the Introduction.
Figures refer to the corpus of illustrations preceding this Catalogue.

PAINTINGS

All measurements are given in inches and in the usual order, first height, then width.

AACHEN, STÄDTISCHES SUERMONDT-MUSEUM

The Queen of Sheba before Solomon. See under Vienna, Gemäldegalerie, No. 175.
Fig. 40.

ADRIA, MUNICIPIO

Portrait of Luigi Grotto, known as " Il cieco d'Adria " (the blind man of Adria). Authenticated
by the letter of thanks from Grotto to Tintoretto, July 17th, 1582 (Lettere famigliari di
Luigi Grotto, Venice 1606, quoted by various authors and more recently in Dedalo, see
below), and by Gasparina Pittoni's engraving of 1589. First reproduced by Mary Pittaluga,
in Dedalo, 1924/25, p. 579.

ALZANO MAGGIORE (BERGAMO), PARISH CHURCH

The Virgin with St. Christopher and two Donors. (136½ × 63.) Originally in the Confrater-
nità dei Mercanti near Madonna dell'Orto, Venice ; disappeared after the dispersal of the
brotherhood in 1819 and reappeared in 1920 at the "Mostra di Pitture dei Secoli XV—
XVIII" (Bergamo). Reproduced in L'Arte XXIII, p. 41, by Mary Pittaluga who dates it
about 1570 and emphatically rejects the attribution to Domenico Tintoretto (Ridolfi II, 257).
Recently attributed by Adolfo Venturi (Storia 9/IV, p. 682) to Domenico and Marco Tintoretto. I have not seen the original.

AMSTERDAM, GOUDSTIKKER COLLECTION

Portrait of a Youth with a book. Formerly in the Galleria Volterra, Florence, and first
reproduced in L'Arte XXX, p. 84, by Mary Pittaluga, who identifies it as the picture mentioned by Ridolfi (II, p. 51) as being in the house of Nicolo Corradino at Padua, "a
youthful student with a cap on his head and a book under his arm." An early work,
about 1560.
Fig. 84.

AMSTERDAM, OTTO LANZ COLLECTION

One of the Muses, playing the viola. Fragment of a lost work, of which the female musi-
cians at Hampton Court are a replica (originally painted for Mantua). Hadeln in
Zeitschr. f. Bild. Kst. 1922/24, July, and Burl. Mag. XLIII, p. 286.
Fig. 108.

AMSTERDAM, OTTO LANZ COLLECTION

The Angel of the Annunciation and the Virgin. Each picture : 44½ × 37½. Wings of an
organ, formerly in San Benedetto, Venice, together with the Christ and the Woman of
Samaria now at the Uffizi. Until 1739 the organ-wings remained in their original
position, in 1746 they were acquired by Algarotti, and later by the Princes Torlonia. The
older authors date them early, Pittaluga (p. 261) "not before 1560."

AMSTERDAM, VOM RATH COLLECTION

The Woman taken in Adultery. An early picture. Bercken-Mayer (I, p. 53, 201) stress the
influence of Schiavone and the antiquated type of composition.
Fig. 15.

AMSTERDAM, HANS TIETJE COLLECTION

Portrait of Ottavio Strada. Long inscription—in which Tintoretto and the year of execution,
1567, are mentioned—added some time later (after 1598). Formerly in the Kaufmann collection, Berlin, then Goldfarb collection, Preussisch Stargard. Probably painted as a pendant
to Titian's portrait of Jacopo Strada in Vienna (Tietze, Titian, coloured plate, opposite
Fig. 273). First reproduced by Hadeln in Jahrb. d. Preuss. Kunstsamml. XLI, p. 32. In my
opinion, painted by Tintoretto's daughter, Marietta. S. Tietze, Venetian Drawings, p. 293.

BERLIN, KAISER-FRIEDRICH-MUSEUM, No. 298 a

The Annunciation. Presented to the Museum in 1899 by Hermann Rosenberg. The catalogue
of the Museum and that of the Mostra (No. 63) date it 1570-80. (Destroyed by fire during the
world war.)
Fig. 170.

BERLIN, KAISER-FRIEDRICH-MUSEUM, No. 300

The Virgin with the Child and the Evangelists Mark and Luke. The catalogue dates it from the 1570's or 1580's. Bercken-Mayer (I, p. 76) are reminded by the figure of the Virgin of Michelangelo's Medici Madonna. A drawing used for the main group in Cambridge, Mass. Fig. 168.

BERLIN, KAISER-FRIEDRICH-MUSEUM, No. 1721

The Miracle of St. Agnes. See under Venice, Madonna dell'Orto.

BERLIN, KAISER-FRIEDRICH-MUSEUM, No. 316

St. Mark with three Procurators of Venice. Inscribed "tres et unus" and "pensate la fin," with the date 1569 beneath the coat-of-arms. Originally in the office of the Camerlenghi at the Rialto, where its pendant was the picture of St. Justina with three Camerlenghi (Venice, Accademia, No. 225). According to Hadeln, Amtliche Berichte XXXII, p. 163, the date is the year in which the three Procurators held office, and the picture ought to be dated somewhat later, about 1571. Fig. 156.

BERLIN, KAISER-FRIEDRICH-MUSEUM, No. 310

Luna with the Horae. Originally part of the decoration executed in 1580 in the hall of the Fondaco dei Tedeschi, on which Paolo Veronese and Palma Giovine also worked. An important late work. Mostra, No. 67. Fig. 177.

BERLIN, KAISER-FRIEDRICH-MUSEUM, No. 298 b

Portrait of an Old Man. Formerly in the Kilényi collection, Budapest. According to Bercken-Mayer (I, p. 67) a late picture, but perhaps it ought to be assigned to the 1560's. Mostra, No. 55. Fig. 81.

BERLIN, KAISER-FRIEDRICH-MUSEUM, No. 299

Portrait of a Procurator. 44 × 37$^{1/2}$. From the Solly collection.

BOLOGNA, PINACOTECA

The Visitation. From the church of San Pietro Martire, Bologna, where Ridolfi and Baldinucci saw it. After the closing of the church in 1863 it was transferred to the Pinacoteca. An early picture, before 1548. Fig. 5.

BOLOGNA, PINACOTECA

The Annunciation. Formerly in S. Matteo, later in S. Isaia. Discovered and publ. by Matteo Marangoni, in Rassegna d'Arte 1901, p. 99. According to Pittaluga, p. 263, a typical shop production. A drawing and a coloursketch preparing the figure of the Virgin, ill. Tietze, Venetian Drawings, Pl. CX, Nos. 1638 and 1725.

BOSTON, MASS., MUSEUM OF FINE ARTS

Portrait of a youth, identified as Alessandro Farnese and publ. by Ph. Hendy in Burl. Mag., 1933. The costume points to c. 1580 which would exclude Alessandro Farnese. The model is perhaps Luigi Gonzaga between his departure for Spain (1581) and his entering the Jesuit order (1585).

BOSTON, MASS., ISABELLA STEWART GARDNER MUSEUM

Portrait of a Lady in black. 45$^{1/4}$ × 37$^{3/4}$. Acquired in 1903 from the Palazzo Chigi, Rome. According to the museum catalogue it is a late work. I included it in my "Masterpieces of European Painting in America" (102), but it seems to me now that it lacks decisive Tintorettesque features.

BREMEN, KUNSTHALLE

Portrait of Doge Francesco Donato. Inscription : F. D. and P. B. (Patriae benemeritus). According to E. Waldmann, who purchased the picture and reproduced it in Cicerone 1930, 325, it was formerly in the Harris collection (as by Titian), and before that perhaps in the collection of Sir Abraham Hume, while it is possible that it may at one time have belonged to King Charles I of England. It can be dated from 1547 to 1553, the years during which this Doge held office. Fig. 78.

BRUNSWICK, MUSEUM, No. 460 a

Aeneas bidding farewell to Dido. Known to have been in the possession of the ducal family from 1778 (Salzdahlum), and at that time had already been given its present name, which is not very clear. Is Aeneas getting out of the boat again to help the fainting Dido? (Hadeln). The stylistic affinity with the Rescue of Arsinoë at Dresden (see below) points to an equally romantic source of the subject. It was first brought to notice by Hadeln in Zeitschr. f. Bild. Kst. 1922/24, July.
Fig. 63.

BRUSSELS, GALLERY, No. 474

Portrait of a young Patrician. $50^{3}/_{8} \times 43^{1}/_{4}$. Transformed into oval shape in the eighteenth century. Ceded by the French government in 1802. An early work, inspired by Titian. First reproduced by Hadeln in Jahrb. d. Preuss. Kunstsamml. 1920, p. 24.

CAËN, MUSEUM, No. 49

The Deposition. According to Thode (Tintoretto, p. 64) a study for a ceiling painting. Stylistically it lies between the Invention of the Cross in Santa Maria Mater Domini and the Crucifixion in San Cassiano, and must therefore have been painted in the 1560's. There is another version in the gallery at Strasbourg (see below), which according to Osmaston is the original. A shop drawing for the figure of Christ in Rotterdam. Tietze, Venetian Drawings, No. 1835.
Fig. 142.

CAMBRIDGE, MASS., FOGG ART MUSEUM

Christ at the Sea of Galilea. 41×45. Formerly G. L. Winthrop Coll., New York. Bercken-Mayer consider this to be Tintoretto's earliest work in which, especially in the formation of the figures, the influence of Parmeggianino is recognizable; the evening seascape with its romantic conception reminds them a little of the creations of the pupils of Giovanni Bellini. To my mind the relationship to Bordone may be more plausible, but on the whole the connection with Tintoretto's years of formation seems doubtful.

CAMBRIDGE, MASS., FOGG ART MUSEUM, ON LOAN FROM THE ARTHUR SACHS COLLECTION

The Baptism of Christ. $76^{3}/_{8} \times 100$. Dated by L. Venturi about 1562-68 (Italian Paintings, Plate 547), while Bercken-Mayer (p. 194) assign it to the mature period, though it is the earliest of Tintoretto's pictures of this subject; the treatment is derived essentially from the traditional iconographic arrangement (Cima in San Giovanni in Bragora, Giovanni Bellini in Santa Corona, Vicenza). The Madrid picture (Prado, No. 397), which in its essential features is a repetition of our painting, is held by Bercken-Mayer (I, 195) to be a school copy, while Hadeln (Jahrb. d. Preuss. Kunstsamml., XLII, p. 82) definitely assigns it to the workshop. Pittaluga (p. 276), who like Hadeln does not discuss its relationship with the Cambridge picture, believes the Prado painting to be a preliminary stage of Tintoretto's picture in San Silvestro, Venice (see below). The Cambridge version too, ill. in my European Masterpieces 99, is only a shop production.

CAMBRIDGE, MASS., FOGG ART MUSEUM, No. 48

Diana as huntress. Formerly belonged to John Ruskin, and afterwards to Arthur Sachs. First reproduced by Perkins in Rassegna d'Arte 1916, p. 25. Generally dated between 1570 and 1580 and unfinished.

CHATSWORTH, COLLECTION OF THE DUKE OF DEVONSHIRE

Samson and Delilah. $62^{1}/_{2} \times 88^{5}/_{8}$. Accepted by Bercken-Mayer (I, p. 181, 268; erroneously described as belonging to the Duke of Westminster) and by Berenson. According to Hadeln (Burl. Mag. LII, p. 21) a workshop repetition, of which a better version is in the Ringling collection at Sarasota, Florida (see below).

CHICAGO, ART INSTITUTE

Tancred baptizing Clorinda. $66^{1}/_{2} \times 45$. Formerly in the Frank G. Logan Coll., Chicago. First published as by Jacopo Tintoretto by Hadeln in Art in America, 1924 June, later on frequently exhibited and published under this name, but a typical work of Domenico Tintoretto, as recognized by Tozzi.

COPENHAGEN, STATENS MUSEUM FER KUNST, No. 30

Portrait of a bearded Man. Acquired in 1913. First brought to notice by Pittaluga in L'Arte 1922, p. 233.

COPENHAGEN, STATENS MUSEUM FER KUNST

Christ and the Woman taken in Adultery. 52 × 95¹/₄. Perhaps identical with the picture of the same subject which Ridolfi (II, 41) saw at Widman's house in Venice and which in 1900 belonged to Carlo Piccoli, Venice (Cantalamessa, Gallerie Nazionali Italiane V, 53). It reached its present location after passing through the Nemes and Heinrich Lanz (Mannheim) collections. It was formerly held to be by Domenico Tintoretto, but Bercken-Mayer have upheld its attribution to Jacopo's early period. The colour scale related to that of the Last Supper in S. Marcuola, Venice, in my opinion, justifies the attribution to Jacopo and the early date.

DETROIT, MICH., INSTITUTE OF FINE ARTS, No. 225

The Dreams of Men. The corners have been bevelled off. Originally a ceiling-painting in the Palazzo Barbo, San Pantaleone, Venice (Ridolfi, II, 55). First reproduced by Hadeln, Art in America XII, p. 27. In view of the stylistic similarity to the ceiling-paintings in the Sala delle Quattro Porte at the Ducal Palace, it may perhaps date from the late 1570's. Fig. 166.

DRESDEN, STAATSGALERIE, No. 559

The Woman taken in Adultery. Identified by Thode (Tintoretto, p. 20) as a picture which Ridolfi (II, p. 46) saw in the house of Vincenzo Zeno. Hadeln (Zeitschr. f. Bild. Kst. XXXIII, p. 28, and Burl. Mag. LI, p. 212), who believes it to be identical with a picture formerly in the collection of the Duke of Buckingham, reproduced it and described it as an important early work, about 1542-45. This opinion has been accepted by Berenson, Bercken-Mayer and others. In Madrid there is a school replica with variations and in reverse (reproduced by Thode, Tintoretto, fig. 3). Fig. 2.

DRESDEN, STAATSGALERIE, No. 266

Battle between St. Michael and Satan. In the gallery since 1754. Accepted by Thode, Osmaston, Bercken-Mayer, and Pittaluga, but Berenson does not mention it, while Loeser (Repertorium XX, p. 333) attributes is to Palma Giovine and believes that it is one of the scenes from the Apocalypse which Palma painted in the Scuola di San Giovanni Evangelista. In my opinion it is an important late work, the subject of which Thode (Tintoretto, p. 126) associates with Tintoretto's predilection in his old age for the miraculous and the mysterious. Fig. 268.

DRESDEN, STAATSGALERIE, No. 269

The Rescue of Arsinoë. Purchased at Mantua in 1743 by Algarotti for King Augustus of Saxony. According to Bercken-Mayer (I, p. 56) a pendant to the so-called Farewell of Aencas at Brunswick. The identification of the subject, which is derived from an Italian edition of Lucan's Pharsalia (the flight of Cleopatra's sister Arsinoë from Alexandria) is due to Wickhoff (Jahrb. d. Preuss. Kunstsamml., 1902, p. 121). Bercken-Mayer's dating about 1550 and Loeser's attribution to Domenico Tintoretto (Repertorium, XX, p. 383) are rejected by Pittaluga (p. 265), who dates the picture about 1570, as does the catalogue of the Mostra (No. 52). To me the types, the colouring and the treatment of space seem to point rather to the 1550's, the period before the Vienna Susanna. Fig. 64.

DRESDEN, STAATSGALERIE, No. 265 a

Portrait of a Lady in mourning. Purchased in 1746 from the ducal gallery in Modena, described in the Dresden inventory of 1754 as the Widow Cornaro. The picture, formerly held to be by Titian and ascribed by Osmaston (II, p. 24) to Paolo Veronese, was first recognized as a work of Tintoretto's by Berenson (Venetian Painters 118) and Loeser, Repertorium, loc. cit., p. 331). Most scholars now consider it an important early work by Tintoretto. Mostra, No. 22. Fig. 79.

DUBLIN, NATIONAL GALLERY OF IRELAND, No. 90

Portrait of a Nobleman. Inscription: 1555 Aetatis 29. Purchased at Christie's, London, in 1866. In bad state of preservation. Described in the 1932 catalogue as a work of the school, but may be by Tintoretto himself. Fig. 80.

DÜSSELDORF, SOHN-RETHEL COLLECTION (formerly)

Portrait of the Procurator Alessandro Gritti. 39 × 29³/₈. Bercken-Mayer (I, p. 67) stress the close stylistic relationship with the self-portrait in the Louvre. From the photograph it certainly appears to be an important work of about 1580.

ESCORIAL

The Washing of Feet. From San Marcuola, Venice. As early as Ridolfi's time it had already left Venice. It was acquired by King Charles I of England and on the sale of his collection after his death went to Spain. Velázquez gave it the place of honour when rearranging the paintings, and other critics (e. g. Morelli in Archivio Storico dell'Arte 1893, p. 280) consider it the best work by Tintoretto in Spain. In San Marcuola there is a copy, which, like the companion-piece, the Last Supper of 1547 (see below) has been enlarged at the top. Osmaston dates it 1545, Pittaluga shortly after 1547; the former date seems to me more likely. A slightly differing version in the collection of Lord Lee of Fareham is described by Bercken-Mayer as a preliminary study (I, p. 264 and II, p. 4), while Pittaluga deems it to be the work of an imitator. As I do not remember the original of this variant, I am inclined to accept Pittaluga's opinion.
Fig. 17.

ESCORIAL

Jesus and Mary Magdalen in the house of Levi. Came originally from Santa Maria Maddalena, Venice, where it is mentioned by Sansovino as early as 1581; as Zanetti, writing in 1771, does not mention it, it probably left when the church was reconstructed during the eighteenth century. Thode (Repertorium für Kunstwissenschaft XXIV, p. 44) was the first to identify it with this picture. Tintoretto's authorship is accepted by Bercken-Mayer and Berenson with reservations; Pittaluga stresses the extensive overpainting. Hadeln (Burl. Mag. XLIII, p. 286) believes the picture to be a workshop replica of a composition of which there is a version dated 1562 in the Museo Civico at Padua (see below).

FLORENCE, PALAZZO PITTI, No. 313

The Virgin and Child in Glory. Mentioned by Baldinucci as being in the Grand-ducal gallery. According to Bercken-Mayer (I, p. 226) probably a fragment of a larger composition, similar to that, obviously of a later period, in the Berlin Museum (see above) or the one in the Accademia at Venice (see below).

FLORENCE, PALAZZO PITTI, No. 3

Venus, Vulcan and Cupid. An early work. Perhaps originally used as a decoration for a bed.
Fig. 6.

FLORENCE, PALAZZO PITTI, No. 83

Portrait of Alvise Cornaro. Formerly attributed by some to Titian, though most are now agreed in assigning it to Tintoretto. As Cornaro, the author of the Vita Sobria, died in 1566 aged 91, the catalogue of the Mostra (No. 42) dates this portrait of a grey-headed old man shortly before that year, while Bercken-Mayer (I, p. 58) assign it to a much earlier period. In view of the treatment and conception, I should be inclined to date it about 1560.
Fig. 151.

FLORENCE, PALAZZO PITTI, No. 131

Portrait of Vincenzo Zeno. Inscription: Vincentius Zeno anno aetatis suae LXXIII. Nobody has yet succeeded in discovering who this particular Zeno was, so that the indication of his age does not help us to date the picture. Mostra, No. 29.

FLORENCE, UFFIZI, No. 8428

God the Father with Adam and Eve at the Tree of Knowledge. Belongs with three other pictures now in the Accademia at Venice to a series which Tintoretto painted in 1550-51 for the Scuola della Trinità near the Salute. The present picture, after a long disappearance, was first brought to notice again by Pittaluga in L'Arte 1922, p. 233.
Fig. 29.

FLORENCE, UFFIZI, Nos. 3497 and 3498

Christ and the Woman of Samaria. Each wing: $45^5/_8 \times 36^5/_8$. Originally the wings of an organ in San Benedetto, Venice, and belonging with the two Annunciation pictures in the Lanz collection, Amsterdam (see above). Were in Count Algarotti's collection in 1776. Purchased in 1910 and first reproduced by Hadeln in Kunstchronik XXII, pp. 388 ff.

FLORENCE, UFFIZI, No. 3084

Leda and the Swan. $63^3/_8 \times 85^3/_4$. Formerly in the collections of Cardinal Mazarin and the Duke of Orleans (E. Ridolfi, Gallerie Nazionali Italiane, I, p. 65). Presented by Mr. Arthur de Noé Walker in 1893. According to Bercken-Mayer an early work, while Pittaluga (p. 267) assigns it to the late period with participation of pupils. This was accepted by Berenson, and in my opinion the share of the shop may be even bigger.
Fig. 57.

FLORENCE, UFFIZI, No. 957

Portrait of Jacopo Sansovino. Borghini mentions the picture as being in Florence in 1584, it having been brought there probably when Sansovino was made a member of the Florentine Academy in 1566. Sansovino was then eighty years old. Hadeln considers that with a view to its destination the picture was adapted to the Florentine style and that it is an atelier work based on a more dramatic version in Weimar, which he holds to be a study from life (Jahrb. der Preuss. Kunstsamml. XLI, p. 38). Another version in the Volterra collection at Florence has been reproduced by G. Fiocco in Dedalo VIII, p. 485. It is perhaps, like the Weimar picture, a replica of the Florence portrait. Mostra, No. 43.
Fig. 155.

FLORENCE, UFFIZI, No. 921

Portrait of a Venetian Admiral. Acquired in 1657 by Cardinal Leopoldo de' Medici. The sitter was formerly supposed to be Sebastiano Veniero, but is more probably Agostino Barbarigo, killed at the Battle of Lepanto in 1571. The dating about 1570 is confirmed by the similarity to the figure of the donor in the Christ in Limbo at San Cassiano, Venice, painted in 1568 (see below).
Fig. 157.

FRANKFORT ON THE MAIN, STAEDELSCHES KUNSTINSTITUT, No. 1521

Moses bringing forth water from the Rock. Acquired in 1914 from the Hamilton collection. While A. Venturi (Storia 9/IV, p. 689) assigns the picture to the workshop, it is by others considered to be by Tintoretto's own hand, painted in the early period about 1544/47, though Hadeln (Burl. Mag. 1922, II, p. 288) assigns it to the end of the 1560's.
Fig. 8.

GHENT, GALLERY

Portrait of Paolo Cornaro delle Anticaglie. Inscription with the date 1561. Sansovino mentions the sitter as being a well-known antiquary. Ridolfi (II, p. 49) saw it in the Zaguri collection, Thode (Tintoretto, p. 80) at Longford Castle, Ireland. It came to Ghent from the Scribe bequest and was at first attributed to Bassano. First published as by Tintoretto by Hadeln (Jahrb. d. Preuss. Kunstsamml. XLI, p. 32).
Fig. 152.

HAMPTON COURT, GALLERY, No. 69

Esther and Ahasuerus. 80¹/₄ × 81¹/₈. It has not been definitely proved that this picture came from Mantua, as it is not mentioned in the inventory of King Charles I's pictures. There is a variant in the Escorial, dated by Bercken-Mayer (I, 50, 182) and Osmaston (I, 179) later than our picture, and held by Pittaluga (p. 269) to be a bad copy with variations. A shop drawing connected with this painting in the Uffizi. Tietze, Venetian Drawings, No. 1792.
Fig. 10.

HAMPTON COURT, GALLERY, No. 77

The Nine Muses. A strip about four inches high has been added at the bottom. Inscription: Jacomo Tentoreto in Venetia. Purchased by King Charles I in Mantua. According to Hadeln a replica of a lost original, of which a fragment has been preserved in the Lanz collection, Amsterdam (see above); while Berenson and Bercken-Mayer (I, 62) mention the considerable participation of the workshop, and the latter also stress the significance of the composition in connection with Tintoretto's efforts to obtain "Grazia." Another version considerably different and including the figure of Apollo, in the G. H. A. Clowes Coll. Indianapolis, Ind., ill. in the cat. of Four Centuries of Venetian Painting, Toledo, Ohio, 1940, No. 56.
Fig. 107.

HAMPTON COURT, GALLERY, No. 113

Portrait of a Nobleman. 41³/₄ × 34¹/₂. Inscribed: An. XXV. 1545. Mentioned in the catalogue of King Charles I's pictures: "Done of Tintoretto's best work, taken for Titian." Crowe and Cavalcaselle assign it to a pupil of Paris Bordone; Klassiker Titian³, 113, to Titian or Titian's school; Berenson, to Titian; Gronau, to Titian, after 1545; Osmaston (II, 18, 19) and Bercken-Mayer (I, 58) to Tintoretto, which to me seems to be right.
Fig. 18.

LEIPZIG, STÄDTISCHES MUSEUM DER BILDENDEN KÜNSTE, No. 239

The Raising of Lazarus. Formerly in the Farrer collection, London. Bercken-Mayer (I, 56, 141, 202) are probably right in dating it shortly before the Miracle of St. Mark of 1548.
Fig. 7.

LENINGRAD, HERMITAGE

Nativity of the Virgin (more correctly : John the Baptist). 72 × 105. Described by Berenson as an atelier work ; by Bercken-Mayer (I, 267) as a school picture or perhaps by Tintoretto's own hand ; Hadeln (Burl. Mag. XLIII, 286) thinks it is an amplified school repetition of the picture in San Zaccaria, Venice (see below), the chief group having been reversed. Hadelns opinion is confirmed by a shop drawing in the Reitlinger Coll., London. Tietze, Venetian Drawings, No. 1846.

LONDON, NATIONAL GALLERY, No. 1130

The Washing of the Feet. Originally in San Trovaso, Venice; sold after 1793 to an English collector and purchased in 1882 at the Hamilton Sale by the National Gallery. As the chapel of the Sacrament in San Trovaso, where the picture hung, was consecrated in 1566, A. L. Mayer, who has given a full description of the picture (Burl. Mag. 1936, I, p. 281), dates it from this year. For stylistic reasons I should be inclined to place it somewhat earlier.
Fig. 139.

LONDON, NATIONAL GALLERY, No. 16

St. George slaying the Dragon. Acquired in 1831. Boschini saw a painting of this subject in the Magistrato del Sale, and Ridolfi (II, 50) another in the house of Senator Pietro Cornaro. The London picture is identified with the second of these. An important work from the 1550's. The drawing belonging thereto in the Louvre is one of the earliest by Tintoretto which have been preserved. Tietze, Venetian Drawings, No. 1738.
Colour plate and figs. 66, 67, 68.

LONDON, NATIONAL GALLERY, No. 1313

The Origin of the Milky Way. From the de Seignelay collection; in Orléans collection, 1727, as the "Nursing of Hercules;" later belonging to Lord Darnley, from whom it was purchased in 1890. Thode (Tintoretto, p. 45) assigns it to the 1540's, with reference to the ceiling-paintings for Pietro Aretino ; Pittaluga (p. 270) dates it after 1570, and Bercken-Mayer (I, 62, 246) about the same date. A drawing in the Accademia, Venice, with the same composition, but with one more figure at the foot, is signed Domenico Tintoretto, for which reason Fogolari (Disegni dell'Accademia di Venezia, p. 22) would ascribe our painting also to Domenico. Recently the problem of this picture has been discussed again by Erna Mandowsky (Burl. Mag. 1938, I, p. 88), who explains the subject as being taken from the Byzantine botanical work, Geoponica. As the same subject also appears on the reverse of a medal of Tommaso Rangoni, it may be assumed that the literary source was connected with this patron of Tintoretto. In this case the picture was probably painted after 1562. In favour of Fogolari's attribution to Domenico on the basis of the latter's drawing in Venice, we have the restlessness and raggedness of the composition, which is contrary to Jacopo's treatment of similar subjects, and the captiousness of the "concetto," which corresponds to the son's predilection for unusual literary subjects. In our opinion, as expoundet in Venetian drawings No. 1552, the drawing is not a study for, but a copy from the painting in London.
Fig. 148.

LONDON, NATIONAL GALLERY, No. 4004

Portrait of Vincenzo Morosini. Presented by the Art Collections Fund in 1924 on the occasion of the National Gallery's Centenary. Reproduced in the same year by MacColl in Burl. Mag., p. 266. Morosini lived from 1511 to 1588 and was Procurator in 1578. The portrait shows him within the last ten years of his life.
Fig. 185.

LONDON, VICTORIA & ALBERT MUSEUM, IONIDES, No. 103

Self-portrait. First brought to notice by Hadeln in Burl. Mag. XLIV, p. 93, who dates it about 1548 and identifies it with a self-portrait of Tintoretto which belonged to the sculptor Alessandro Vittoria (Predelli, Le memorie e carte di Alessandro Vittoria, in Archivio Trentino XXIII, p. 233). Bercken (Zeitschr. f. Bild. Kst. 59, p. 330) doubts the authenticity of the picture, but admits that the features agree with the self-portrait of the grey-haired Tintoretto in the Louvre (see below). The similarity of conception and model at a distance of four decades seems to me convincing. — Another replica, seemingly also an original, formerly in the Norton Coll., Boston, now at Wildenstein's, New York, ill. Four Centuries of Venetian Painting, Toledo, Ohio, 1941, No. 57.
Fig. 1.

LONDON, P. and D. COLNAGHI

S. Roch taken prisoner. Sketch of the painting in the church of S. Rocco, Venice (s. below). Important as one of the few existing sketches of a whole composition by Tintoretto. Fig. 286.

LONDON, BRIDGEWATER HOUSE, No. 40

The Entombment. Strips have been added on all four sides. Probably the same picture that Vasari and Sansovino mention as being in the Cappella Bassi at San Francesco della Vigna, which was fully described by Ridolfi and engraved by Jacob Matham in 1594 (in reverse) (Osmaston II, 183). Even in Ridolfi's time the picture had been cut of its frame, leaving only an angel with the crown of thorns (Thode, Repertorium, XXIV, p. 442). To judge by the style, painted in the 1560's. Fig. 141.

LONDON, FORMERLY IN THE COLLECTION OF SIR W. BROMLEY-DAVENPORT

The Contest between Apollo and Marsyas. Obviously identical with the ceiling-painting of this subject which Tintoretto painted in 1545, together with a lost Mercury and Argus, for Aretino, as we learn from the latter's letter of thanks written in February of that year (Lettere IV, 110). Later, perhaps as early as 1618, was in English possession and subsequently belonged to the Duke of Abercorn. It was included in Christie's sale of Sir W. Bromley-Davenport's collection on July 28th and 29th, 1926. First brought to notice by Hadeln (Burl. Mag. 1922, II, 206); he compares the pose of Apollo with that of the male figure in a drawing of Tintoretto's at Christ Church, Oxford (Hadeln, Tintoretto's Drawings, Plate I) and also maintains that other figures were based on sculptured models. All of Hadeln's conclusions fail to convince us, as explained in our Venetian Drawings, p. 271 and 275. Fig. 3.

LONDON, R. SMITH-BARRY COLLECTION

Group-portrait of the Pellegrina Family. Among the more recent writers Bercken-Mayer (I, 260) and Osmaston (II, 25 and 121) mention the picture, but do not reproduce it; both recognize it as the family portrait of the Pellegrina's described in detail by Ridolfi (II, 55). At one time belonged to Lord Barrymore. The picture, the original of which I have not seen, has many features which make it difficult to believe that it is entirely by Tintoretto's hand. The most likely date for it would be during the 1560's. Fig. 150.

LÜBECK, KATHARINENMUSEUM

The Raising of Lazarus. Inscribed: Jacomo Tintoretto Inventor—A. 1576 Venezia. From the inscription alone we may conclude—as Pittaluga (p. 272) has done—that the execution was due mainly to the workshop, whose participation is recognizable in details, while the rhythm of the linear composition points to Tintoretto having been the designer. Perhaps there was on original version in the 1550's. On the noteworthy influence which the picture exercised on painting in Lübeck, see Theodor Riewerts, Der Maler Joh. Willinger in Lübeck, in Zeitschrift des deutschen Vereins für Kunstwissenschaft, 1936, p. 282. Fig. 165.

LUCCA, CATHEDRAL

The Last Supper. Mentioned in the earlier literature and held by Pittaluga (p. 273) to be a work of the last period, with participation of the workshop, already finished in 1592, as we possess a document of that time stating that it was intended to transfer the picture to another altar. I have not re-examined the original lately.

LYONS, MUSEUM, No. 45

Danaë. Presented by the State in 1811. Generally attributed to Tintoretto and dated 1555-60 but Pittaluga (p. 270) assigns it to Domenico Tintoretto, which seems highly convincing to me. Mostra, No. 25. Fig. 60.

MADRID, PRADO

386. *The chaste Susanna.*
388. *Esther and Ahasuerus.*
389. *Judith and Holofernes.*

394. *The Queen of Sheba before Solomon.*
395. *Joseph and Potiphar's Wife.*
396. *The Finding of Moses.*

These six pictures have obviously always belonged together and must have formed a
continuous frieze in a room or on a bed-canopy. To judge by the perspective they must
have been inclined towards the front. If, as the Prado catalogue states, the Purification
of the Virgins of Midian (see below) formed, together with these six pictures, a complete
series when Velázquez purchased them in Venice, it must have been painted subsequently,
for this large picture is undoubtedly of later origin than the six small ones. (Others
identify this series as one which Tintoretto, according to Ridolfi II, 50, painted for Philip II.)
The six pictures are generally held to be youthful works, but can hardly have been painted
before the end of the 1550's.
Fig. 101—106.

MADRID, PRADO, No. 393

The Purification of the captured Virgins of Midian (Numbers, XXXI). 76³/4 × 71¹/4. Purchased
by Velázquez at Venice for Philip IV, and at that time described as the Gathering of
Manna. Thode and Osmaston date it about 1570, as does Pittaluga (p. 275), though the
latter—like Berenson and Philipps—on account of the hardness and exactitude of the
execution is inclined to doubt that it is by Tintoretto's own hand. The existence of a
drawing by Jacopo Tintoretto (in the former F. Königs Coll., Tietze, Venetian Drawings,
No. 1662) used in reverse for this painting, is a further argument in support of workshop
participation. The relationship of the types to those of the Berlin Luna makes it possible
to date the picture as late as 1580.

MADRID, PRADO, No. 391

Judith and Holofernes. Known to have been in Madrid since 1772. According to Hadeln
(Burl. Mag. 1922, p. 227), with whom Bercken-Mayer agree, an early picture; according to
Pittaluga (p. 273), a late work, executed with the help of pupils. The most likely date
seems to me to be in the 1550's.
Fig. 58.

MADRID, PRADO, No. 390

Judith and Holofernes. 78 × 128. According to the Prado catalogue, may have been purchased
by Velázquez in Venice. Most writers assign it to Tintoretto's late or very late period,
but Pittaluga (p. 275) holds it to be an imitation of Tintoretto's style. In view of the
impossibility of examining the picture again, I will limit myself to remarking that to judge
by the photograph, the mixture of comparatively early features with a landscape tallying
with the later period, seems to give weight to this opinion. The drawing in the British
Museum (Tietze, Venetian Drawings, No. 1835), which Hadeln believed to be a study
for the corpse of Holofernes in this picture, is in reality the immediate preliminary study
for the body of Christ in the Deposition at Caën (see above). This disposes of yet another
argument in favour of the authenticity of the Madrid picture.

MADRID, PRADO, No. 398

So-called Sketch for the Paradise. 66¹/8 × 214¹/2. Purchased for Spain by Velázquez during
his second journey to Italy, and for this reason alone not identical with the sketch of a
Last Judgement for King Philip II, on which Tintoretto was working in 1587, according
to a letter of the ambassador Hieronymus Lipomanno (L'Arte 1922, p. 94). Except for a
few variations, the composition agrees with that of Tintoretto's Paradise in the Sala del
Gran Consiglio in the Ducal Palace. Since Pittaluga, who at one time supported the theory
that it was by Tintoretto's own hand, now admits that it is derived from the Paradise in
the Ducal Palace, it can be definitely excluded from Tintoretto's works.

MADRID, PRADO, No. 399

Naval Battle (also known as "The Rape of Helen"). Purchased by Velázquez in Venice for
King Philip IV. Beroqui's supposition that this picture is identical with a Battle against
the Turks that Tintoretto painted in 1562 for Cardinal Ercole Gonzaga is contradicted by the
late style; it might, however, be the other battle picture of this type mentioned in a
Mantuan inventory dated 1607. That for this picture a drawing was used, which had
already been used for the Oxford Martyrdom of St. Lawrence (see below), a picture which
is stylistically of an earlier period, would be a confirmation of the participation of the
workshop in the execution. Tietze, Venetian Drawings, No. 1677.
Fig. 245.

MADRID, PRADO, No. 392

Tarquin and Lucrece. 74 × 106³/4. According to the Madrid catalogue, this picture was
altered by Luca Giordano and subsequently restored again to its original form. In any

case it has suffered damage and is now usually kept in the repository of the Prado. Hadeln was the first to bring it to notice in Burl. Mag. 1922, II, p. 206, and described it as a kind of pendant to the Munich Venus, Vulcan and Cupid (see below), dating from the 1540's. He sees sculptural reminiscences, especially in the pose of Lucrece, which he thinks is borrowed from the nude on the left of Michelangelo's Erythraean Sibyl, but this does not seem convincing to me. The composition seems to be based on the more concise and dramatic version in the R. Goetz Coll., New York (see below), and, in view of the construction of space (as in the Marriage of Cana, Venice, Santa Maria della Salute, see below) to make a later date—in the 1560's—more probable.

MADRID, PRADO, No. 378

Portrait of a Gentleman with a golden chain. In the possession of the Spanish royal family since 1686. Attributed by Alende-Salazar and Sanchez Cantón to Paolo Veronese; by Berenson, Osmaston and Bercken-Mayer to Tintoretto and assigned by them to about 1550 which seems to me likely.
Fig. 75.

MADRID, PRADO, No. 379

Portrait of a Venetian Senator. 30¼ × 24¾. The catalogue says that the sitter resembles Vincenzo Zeno, but this is incorrect. To judge by the style, painted in the 1570's.
Fig. 182.

MADRID, PRADO, No. 366

Supposed portrait of Sebastiano Venier. 32¼ × 26⅜. Inscribed: "Sebastiano Veniero," on a tablet which, for compositional reasons alone, seems to be a later addition. The identification of the sitter, who has no resemblance to the authenticated portraits of Venier, has not yet been possible. Painted in the late 1570's or the early 1580's.
Fig. 181.

MILAN, BRERA, No. 234b

The Finding of St. Mark's Body. One of the three scenes from the legend of St. Mark which Tommaso Rangone of Ravenna commissioned Tintoretto to paint in 1562 for the Scuola Grande di San Marco; it was praised by Vasari, Sansovino and the other old authors. After its transfer to the Brera in 1811, this painting from 1847 on was deposited for several decades in the church of San Marco in Milan. Two drawings (Tietze, Venetian Drawings, Nos. 1692 and 1711) prepare figures in this painting while another in Frankfort (Tietze l.c., No. 1819), connected with it by Ricci, Hadeln and Pittaluga, is nearer to a school painting in Basle (Öffentliche Kunstsammlung, No. 115, ill. C. Ricci, La Pinacoteca di Brera, p. 7) of the Body of Christ between two Angels. Our picture shows the moment when the Venetians are letting down the body of the Saint, and the latter appears to them and tells them to desist from further search. It is impossible to suppose—as Voll does (Entwicklungsgeschichte der Malerei II, 170 ff.)—that the body lying on the ground is that of the Saint; it is more likely to be that of the dead Claudius, who was removed from his grave in order to be placed as a substitute in the sarcophagus of St. Mark (Bercken-Mayer I, 238)
Mostra, No. 35.
Fig. 112.

MILAN, BRERA, No. 217

Pietà. Painted for a lunette in the courtyard of the Procuratie di Sopra, Tintoretto being paid 25 ducats for it on February 19th, 1563. In 1590 the picture was restored by Tintoretto, when it was transferred to the new Scamozzi building together with other pictures by Paolo Veronese and Marco del Moro. It was brought to Milan in 1808.
Mostra, No. 39.
Fig. 119.

MILAN, CASTELLO SFORZESCO

St. Helena with other Saints. 108¼ × 65. Originally in San Marcuola, Venice. Mentioned as being in Santa Croce, Milan, in 1776. Transferred to the Brera in 1805, as by Paolo Veronese. Painted in the 1560's.
Fig. 89.

MILAN, CASTELLO SFORZESCO

Portrait of Jacopo Soranzo. The sitter became Procurator in 1522 and died in 1551, aged 85. The catalogue of the Mostra (No. 10) dates it shortly before 1551, on convincing grounds.
Fig. 82.

MUNICH, ÄLTERE PINAKOTHEK, No. 1130

Christ in the house of Martha and Mary. Came from the Dominican church in Augsburg. The catalogue of the Mostra (No. 51), following that of the Pinakothek and Thode (Tintoretto, p. 110) assigns it to the decade between 1570 and 1580. Bercken-Mayer (I, 201) rightly point out that the scene is derived from St. Luke x. 10.
Colour plate.

MUNICH, ÄLTERE PINAKOTHEK

Venus, Vulcan and Cupid. Formerly in the Kaulbach collection, Munich; before that in Paris, and still earlier in the Munro collection in England. Waagen (Treasures II, 134) gives a full description of it, as Hadeln notes when correcting his earlier statement that it came from Peter Lely's collection (Burl. Mag. LII, p. 21). Hadeln (Burl. Mag. 1922, December) and Bercken-Mayer assign it to the early period, Pittaluga (p. 280) and, following her, the catalogue of the Mostra (No. 66) to the late period, about 1580; Pittaluga assumes the participation of pupils. She also assigns the Berlin drawing (Tietze, Venetian Drawings, No. 1561), the compositional sketch for our picture, to Tintoretto's late period. Her remarks do not seem to me quite convincing, though I should not go so far back as Bercken-Mayer, who try to relate the picture to Tintoretto's friendship with Aretino about 1545. Spatial construction, types and colouring seem to me to point to about 1555; Titian's contemporary Andromeda (Tietze, Titian, 230) may have provided inspiration for the body of Venus, while the composition as a whole may have got inspiration from Daniele da Volterra's " Mercury and Aeneas. "
Fig. 56.

MUNICH, ÄLTERE PINAKOTHEK, Nos. 7302 to 7309

The Gonzaga Cycle.

> First Series : 1. The Investiture of Giovanni Francesco Gonzaga.
> 2. The Battle on the Adige.
> 3. The Relief of Legnago by Frederick I.
> 4. The Battle on the Taro.

> Second Series : 1. The Capture of Milan.
> 2. The Capture of Parma.
> 3. The Capture of Pavia.
> 4. Philip IV's Entry into Mantua.

The first series was painted shortly before 1579 for Mantua, by order of Duke Guglielmo Gonzaga, the second in 1579-80. The complete cycle, which in 1709 appeared in the inventory of the estate of the last Duke of Mantua, who died one year before, is found in the inventory of the castle of Schleissheim in 1748, but after this it was dispersed. In 1895 it was brought together again, and after restoration was hung at Schleissheim and in 1909 in the Pinakothek. From the documents published by A. Luzio (Fasti Gonzagheschi dipinti dal Tintoretto, in Archivio Storico dell'Arte III, p. 392) we learn that a detailed literary programme was sent to the painter and that he had to submit designs, which were carefully checked as regards their historical accuracy. That assistants took part in the execution is certain, as is shown by the schematic manner in which the master's motives— e. g. the soldier falling forwards with outstretched arms in the Battle on the Adige—are executed in reverse and with variations (E. Tietze-Conrat in Die Graph. Künste, new series, I, p. 91). Tintoretto alone, however, is responsible for the conception, some of which is magnificent. Several drawings (Tietze, Venetian Drawings, Nos. 1571, 1626, 1642, 1719, 1724, 1727) are preparations for this series, among them the magnificent sketch in Naples for the "Battle on the Taro" (s. Fig. 219).
Figs. 220-224.

NEW YORK, METROPOLITAN MUSEUM, 13.75

The Miracle of the Loaves and Fishes. Purchased in 1913. Dated by Hadeln in the 1560's (Burl. Mag. 1922, II, p. 288); by Bercken-Mayer, 1544 to 1547. The latter stress the influence of Parmeggianino and the points of contact with Schiavone. The relationship to "Moses striking the Rock" in Frankfort is rightly stressed by the museum's catalogue.
Fig. 9.

NEW YORK, METROPOLITAN MUSEUM, 10.206

Doge Alvise Mocenigo in prayer before the Redeemer. Formerly in the collections of Baron Rumohr, John Ruskin and Mrs. Arthur Severn. A preliminary study for the corresponding votive painting in the Sala del Collegio at the Ducal Palace, the execution of which, since Thode (Repertorium XXIV, p. 28), has been generally attributed to the workshop. Escher

(Repertorium XLI, p. 96) also draws attention to the fact that this mural painting has been disfigured more than any of the others by overpainting, while the New York sketch is far more grandiose with its better defined accentuation and combination of the different groups. The sketch is dated between 1577 and 1584, during which years Mocenigo was in office. It is an important piece of evidence for Tintoretto's share in the great official commissions of this late period.
Fig. 234.

NEW YORK, METROPOLITAN MUSEUM, No. 39.55

The Finding of Moses. Unfinished. Formerly in the collection of G. D. Leslie, R. A., London, who acquired it in 1856. Though dated about 1570 by L. Venturi (Italian Paintings, pl. 549) more likely from the 1550's, as suggested by A. L. Mayer, and accepted by the catalogue of the museum.
Fig. 287.

NEW YORK, COLLECTION OF GENERAL JOHN ROSS DELAFIELD

Portrait of Doge Pietro Loredan. According to the owner, an old family heirloom. Ridolfi mentions a portrait of this Doge as being in the house of Giovanni Francesco Loredan. Probably painted while the Doge was in office, i. e. 1567-1570, as G. Lorenzetti supposed when he first drew attention to the picture (Dedalo 1925/26, p. 310). I have not seen the original.
Fig. 154.

NEW YORK, FRICK COLLECTION

Portrait of the Procurator Nicolò Priuli (?). Formerly in the collection of the Duke of Abercorn. By some critics considered a late autograph (see L. Venturi, Italian Paintings in America, II, Plate 564), in my opinion rather by an contemporary imitator of Tintoretto's late style.
Fig. 184.

NEW YORK, PIERPONT MORGAN LIBRARY

Portrait of a Moor. 40×35. Formerly in the Marquis of Dufferin Coll. Publ. by L. Venturi in Italian Paintings, pl. 556 and T. Borenius, in Pantheon 1930, February, and dated 1570—75.

NEW YORK, RICHARD GOETZ COLL.

Tarquin and Lucrece. Canvas. This imposing painting, of which a widened version in the Prado was published by Hadeln in 1922 (see Madrid, Prado, No. 392), is one of Jacopo Tintoretto's most powerful compositions of profane subjects. Both, the rendering of the bodies related to the "Pool of Bethesda", in the church of San Rocco, Venice, of 1559, and that of space reminding of the "Marriage at Cana" in Santa Maria della Salute, Venice, finished not before 1557 (see below) point to a date of origin in the late 1550's. Some features are somewhat bewildering: on one hand the emphasis laid on realistic detail (as for instance the statues holding the curtain one of which has been turned over in the struggle, and, furthermore, the pearls dropping from the broken necklace) is typical of Tintoretto's early period. On the other hand, the brushwork in some spots is so broad as usually in Tintoretto's later years. The latter may be due to later retouches.
Fig. 285.

NEW YORK, FORMERLY IN THE EHRICH GALLERIES

Portrait of a Venetian Nobleman with a Page. Inscribed: Aetatis suae XD (instead of XL)— Jacomo Tento. fece MDLXI. On the basis of a portrait medal Hill identified the sitter as Scipione Clusoni (Burl. Mag. 1915, I, p. 66), but Hadeln (Jahrb. d. Preuss. Kunstsamml. XLI, Plate 60, p. 32) rejected this. The picture is highly esteemed by Bercken-Mayer (I, 58, 259 f.), who see in it, in contrast to the consciously clear expression of Titian's portraits, traces of that general tendency to adapt the expression to moods which is characteristic of early Cinquecento Venetian portraiture. Hadeln (Burl. Mag. XLIII, 286) thinks that in this case too the detailed inscription points to a participation of the workshop. The painting is mentioned by Pittaluga, but not by L. Venturi and Berenson.

OXFORD, CHRIST CHURCH, No. 213

The Martyrdom of St. Lawrence. Guise donation. In the collection (Catalogue by Borenius, 1916) described as a school work, but Hadeln maintains (Burl. Mag. XLVIII, p. 115) that it is by Tintoretto's own hand and he identifies it with the "small picture" of this subject which (according to Ridolfi, II, p. 52) was commissioned by the Bononi family for San Francesco della Vigna, Venice, but was rejected and afterwards passed into the possession of the Procurator Morosini. Hadeln dates the picture, which must be derived from Titian's

painting of the same subject, and more precisely from the later version in the Escorial, in
the 1570's. Several drawings (Tietze, Venetian Drawings, Nos. 1682, 1677, 1700) served
for figures in this painting, and one of them (No. 1677) was used a second time in the
Naval Battle at the Prado (s. above).
Fig. 169.

PADUA, MUSEO CIVICO, No. 670

Christ in the house of the Pharisee. Signed: Jacome Tintoreto 1562. Osmaston was the first
writer to mention the picture, and afterwards Hadeln (Burl. Mag. XLIII, p. 286) drew
attention to its superiority to a similar composition, amplified and arranged in breadth, in
the Escorial, which is probably merely a workshop replica. But the Padua copy also reveals
weaknesses, which make it improbable that Tintoretto executed the whole of it himself.
This seems to be another confirmation of the fact that Tintoretto's signed pictures were
mostly destined for provincial patrons, and probably for that reason their execution was left
mainly to assistants.
Fig. 109.

PARIS, LOUVRE, No. 1464

Susanna bathing. Seen by Ridolfi (II, p. 45) in Casa Barbarigo. Purchased in 1684 by the
Marquis Hauterive. Painted between 1555 and 1560, probably before the Vienna version of the same subject. Northern assistants may have executed some of the accessories,
which are as plentiful as in a still-life.
Fig. 59.

PARIS, LOUVRE, No. 1496

Paradise. Mentioned by Ridolfi (II, p. 52) as being in the collection of the Counts Bevilacqua,
Verona, where Goethe also saw it; shortly afterwards it was taken away by the French.
Its relationship to Tintoretto's huge picture in the Ducal Palace has been amply discussed
by Hadeln (Jahrb. d. Preuss. Kunstsamml. XL, p. 119); he makes it clear that this is not
a sketch made immediately before the execution of the "Paradiso", but a model for
the competition in 1579. The much greater freedom of this model in comparison with the
actual picture may be explained by the fact that the latter was altered in response to the
wishes of the authorities who commissioned it.
Figs. 244, 242.

PARIS, LOUVRE, No. 1466

Self-portrait. Inscription added later: IACOBUS - TENTORETUS - PICTOR - VENE-
TIANUS - IPSIUS - F. On the engraving of the picture made by Gisbert van Geen in
1588, for which Pozzoserrato supplied the ornamental framework and which Ridolfi
reproduced in his biography, Tintoretto is described as being seventy years old. According
to this the picture must have been painted about 1588, with which the style and the age
of the sitter agree. From a letter to Francesco Gonzaga, written in 1612 and published by
A. Luzio (Galleria dei Gonzaga, p. 110), in which among others a self-portrait of Tintoretto
is offered to him, Pittaluga (p. 288) argues that the Paris picture may have been the one in
question. Hadeln (Jahrb. d. Preuss. Kunstsamml. XLI, p. 32) mentions another portrait
which might have been the one mentioned and which formed part of Rubens's estate. The
copy of the Paris portrait, his favourite picture, which Manet painted in 1867, is now in the
museum at Dijon.
Frontispiece.

PARIS, LOUVRE, SCHLICHTING COLLECTION

Portrait of a Venetian Admiral. 46 × 36¹/₄. The picture was formerly described as a portrait
of Vincenzo Cappello by Titian, which would mean that it was painted about 1540.
A. L. Mayer (Gazette des Beaux-Arts 1934, II, p. 223) maintains resolutely that it was
painted by Tintoretto about 1570 and represents Sebastiano Venier although B. Berenson
(in Festschrift für Max J. Friedländer, 1927, p. 228 ff.) had identified it as by Palma Giovine
and a portrait of another admiral, Nicola Cappello. In my opinion Berenson is right.

PRINCETON, N. J., MUSEUM OF HISTORIC ART.

Poet in Landscape? Formerly (1773) in the Palazzo Poggio Cajano, Florence. Exhibited as
St. John at Patmos in "Four Centuries of Venetian Paintings", in Toledo, Ohio, 1940, No. 55.
A sketch possibly from Tintoretto's late period, in view of some resemblance to the Mount
of Olives, in Santo Stefano, Venice.
Fig. 289.

RICHMOND, COLLECTION OF SIR HERBERT COOK, Bart.

Portrait of a Venetian Senator. The dating in the 1570's (Bercken-Mayer I, 67, 259: about 1580) is supported by the close resemblance to the so-called self-portrait of 1573 in San Rocco (Fig. 179).
Fig. 180.

RIESE (TREVISO), PARISH CHURCH

The Espousal of the Virgin. Originally in Santa Maria Maggiore, Venice, together with the Adoration of the Magi and the Rejection of Joachim's Sacrifice, which are now in San Trovaso (see below). According to Pittaluga, who rediscovered it after it had already been brought to notice by Andrea Baretta in 1842, it is a late work with participation of Domenico and perhaps also of Marco Tintoretto. I have not seen the original.

ROCHESTER, N. Y., GEORGE EASTMAN COLLECTION, UNIVERSITY OF ROCHESTER

Portrait of a Venetian Senator. Formerly in the collection of the Duke of Abercorn and a companion-piece to the portrait in the Frick Collection, New York, and highly rated by some writers. See L. Venturi, Italian Paintings in America, Plate 563. Like the companion-piece probably by a follower of Tintoretto.
Fig. 183.

ROME, GALLERIA NAZIONALE, No. 5144

The Woman taken in Adultery. Perhaps the version of this subject which in Ridolfi's time (II, p. 41) belonged to Vincenzo Zeno. Presented to the gallery by Principe Chigi. First recognized by Adolfo Venturi. Generally held to be an early work, before 1548. Mostra, No. 5.
Fig. 14.

ROME, GALLERIA COLONNA, No. 17

Hylus and Narcissus. $58 \times 74^{3}/4$. With the exception of Bercken-Mayer (I, p. 268), who are reminded of Schiavone, all investigators recognize this picture as by Tintoretto, as does also the catalogue of the Mostra, No. 21. The possibilities of comparison afforded by the Mostra, however, tended to confirm the doubts as to its authenticity.

ROME, GALLERIA COLONNA, No. 6

The Adoration of the Holy Ghost. $43^{1}/4 \times 34^{5}/8$. Of the two versions of this subject which Boschini mentions he attributes that in the Magistrato della Sanità to Parrasio Michele, and that in the Magistrato dei Camerlenghi to Domenico Tintoretto. Pittaluga (p. 284) is inclined to think that the Rome picture is Domenico's, though the portraits remind her of Jacopo. Accepted as a late work of Jacopo's by Berenson and Bercken-Mayer, and reproduced by the latter (Plate 172). Pittaluga's supposition seems to me more correct.

ROME, GALLERIA DORIA, No. 386

So-called Portrait of Jansenius. $47^{1}/4 \times 39^{3}/4$. That the sitter could not be Cornelius Janssen, Bishop of Ypres, was rightly asserted by Crowe and Cavalcaselle, who attributed the picture to Titian, in which they were followed by Fischel, Klassiker der Kunst, 3rd edition, 196, Basch and other writers. Berenson, who describes it as a portrait of Cardinal Cristoforo Madruzzo, Thode and especially Pittaluga (Dedalo 1925, February) consider it to be an early work by Tintoretto. Neither of these attributions is completely satisfactory.

SALISBURY, WILTON HOUSE

The Washing of Feet. First mentioned, as by Tintoretto, in 1731, in Carlo Gambarini's Description of the Earl of Pembroke's Paintings. Reproduced in Burl. Mag. LXI, 99, by Tancred Borenius, who stresses the affinity with Titian's palette and to a certain extent with Bonifazio's composition; he dates it about 1545, shortly before the Washing of Feet in the Escorial.
Fig. 16.

SANDS POINT, L. I., N. Y., L. M. RABINOWITZ COLL.

Portrait of a Man. Published by L. Venturi, The Rabinowitz Coll., New York, 1945, pl. XXIV, and correctly dated c. 1570.
Fig. 284.

SAN FRANCISCO, PALACE OF THE LEGION OF HONOUR

The Virgin, recumbent, with the Child. Signed: Jacopo Tentoreto. Lionello Venturi (Italian Paintings in America, Plate 548) dates it together with the Presentation of the Virgin in Madonna dell'Orto about 1560. Probably a fragment of a larger composition, in which the workshop, as also the signature leads me to suppose, also participated. Fig. 69.

SARASOTA, FLORIDA, THE JOHN AND MABLE RINGLING MUSEUM OF ART

Samson and Delilah. Hadeln calls this picture, which is mentioned by Berenson, but not by L. Venturi, a version by Tintoretto's own hand of a composition of which an amplified version is in the collection of the Duke of Devonshire at Chatsworth (Burl. Mag. LII, p. 21). I have not seen the original.

SCHLEISSHEIM, GEMÄLDEGALERIE, No. 991

Crucifixion. See Venice, Scuola di San Rocco, *Crucifixion.*

STRASBOURG, MUSEUM

Deposition from the Cross. The picture is a variant of the one in Caën (s. Fig. 142) which A. L. Mayer dates by at least five years earlier than the Strasbourg version, which he published in Gazette des Beaux-Arts, 1945, February, p. 85.

TURIN, ROYAL GALLERY, No. 576

The Trinity. Came from Palazzo Durazzo, Genoa. Recognized by Thode (Repertorium, XXIV, p. 443) and Pittaluga (Arte 1919, p. 223) as a fragment of an altar-piece which was formerly in San Girolamo, Venice (Boschini, p. 453; Ridolfi, II, p. 33). On the other hand Baudi de Vesme (1909 catalogue, p. 156) and Bercken-Mayer (I, p. 230) think that it is not a fragment, but a complete composition, perhaps a ceiling-painting. Pittaluga's exhaustive arguments seem to me convincing, as does her dating, about 1570-75. Fig. 172.

VENICE, ACCADEMIA

The Creation of the Animals. Together with the two following pictures (The Fall of Man; Cain and Abel), the Adam and Eve at the Tree of Knowledge in the Uffizi (see above) and the (lost) Creation of Man, belonging to a series which Borghini described in the Scuola della Trinità near the Salute; according to G. Ludwig (Jahrb. der Kunsthist. Samml. XXVI, p. 103), the cycle was painted in 1550-51. That it dates from Tintoretto's early period is in any case certain. The picture was rediscovered by Hadeln in the repository of the Ducal Palace, and reproduced by him in Zeitschr. f. Bild. Kunst., new series, XXXIII, p. 93. Mostra, No. 17. Fig. 28.

VENICE, ACCADEMIA, No. 43

The Fall of Man. Origin and dating as for the preceding. Zucchi's engraving shows that the picture has been cut at the right side. The style of the figures has been most exhaustively discussed by Bercken-Mayer, and its place in Tintoretto's landscape-painting by Pittaluga in L'Arte XXIII, p. 163. Earlier Ridolfi (p. 18) had used this painting as an example of Tintoretto's studies after sculpture. Fig. 30.

VENICE, ACCADEMIA, No. 41

Cain and Abel. Origin and dating as for the preceding. Bercken-Mayer refer to Schiavone's Samson in Palazzo Pitti; more important, perhaps, is the influence of Titian's ceiling in the Salute. This picture also, as can be seen from Zucchi's engraving, has been cut on the right side. Mostra, No. 16. Fig. 31.

VENICE, ACCADEMIA, No. 725

The Presentation in the Temple. From the sacristy of the Jesuit church, where it is mentioned by Sansovino, Borghini and Ridolfi, the last-named adding that it was painted in competition with Schiavone. According to Berenson an early work, and this is confirmed by Bercken-Mayer with reference to the very close similarity to the Presentation of the Virgin in Madonna dell'Orto, which enables them to date it definitely in the 1550's. Fig. 97.

VENICE, ACCADEMIA, No. 232

The Woman taken in Adultery. 45¾×80. Thode, who first had doubted its authenticity (Tintoretto, p. 20), recognized it as an early work in Repertorium XXIV, p. 8. In this he is followed by Berenson and Bercken-Mayer. The picture is in a bad state of preservation, which spoils the impression. Nevertheless it might be a youthful work by Tintoretto.

VENICE, ACCADEMIA, No. 213

The Crucifixion. From the demolished church of San Severo, Venice. The identification of this picture was first made by Thode, who although Ridolfi dates it from the early period, maintained that it was painted at the beginning of the 1560's, just before the Crucifixion in San Rocco. Bercken-Mayer, on the other hand, date it from the 1550's. (For two drawings connected with this painting, one in the Uffizi, the other in Windsor, s. Tietze, Venetian Drawings, Nos. 1633, 1759.)
Fig. 117.

VENICE, ACCADEMIA, No. 217

The Entombment. From the disused Chiesa dell'Umiltà, where the picture was seen by Boschini; Pittaluga's supposition that this was the Entombment mentioned by Vasari and Ridolfi as being in Santa Maria della Carità is rejected by the catalogue of the Mostra (No. 31) with good reasons. Thode (Repertorium XXIV, p. 9) dates it about 1560, and this dating is to be preferred to others, taking into account Bercken-Mayer's emphasis on its closeness to the Crucifixion in the Gesuiti.
Fig. 118.

VENICE, ACCADEMIA, No. 210

The Virgin with the Child, Saints Mark, Theodore, Sebastian and Roch and three Chamberlains. Inscribed: Unanimi Concordiae Simbolus 1566, with the arms of the Pisani, Malipiero and Dolfin families. Originally in the Magistrato dei Camerlenghi at the Rialto, later in Santi Giovanni e Paolo. An important example of official portraiture from Tintoretto's middle period with ample participation of Domenico, as also suggested by A. Venturi, Storia 9/IV, Fig. 671.
Fig. 149.

VENICE, ACCADEMIA, No. 221

The Virgin with the Child, Saints Marina (not Anthony), Cecilia, Theodore, Cosmas and Damian. From the abandoned church of Santi Cosma e Damiano on the Giudecca. On account of the compositional transformation of the theme of the Santa Conversazione and the prominence of the silhouette effects, many writers consider this to be one of the chief works of the 1570's; Berenson assumes a certain participation of assistants, while A. Venturi (Storia 9/IV, pp. 685 ff.) gives a large share of the work to Marietta.
Fig. 175.

VENICE, ACCADEMIA, No. 243

The Virgin with the Child and four Senators. Originally in the Magistrato del Sale. According to Boschini, our picture was the middle panel between the two others showing St. Andrew and St. Jerome, and St. George and St. Louis. The Virgin has been much overpainted, which spoils the effect. A drawing in Cambridge, Mass., is used in the painting. Tietze, Venetian Drawings, No. 1575.
Fig. 83.

VENICE, ACCADEMIA

St. Andrew and St. Jerome. St. Louis of Toulouse and St. George with the Princess. Originally in the Magistrato del Sale (Salt Office) to which the two pictures were presented by officials in 1552. In 1777 they were transferred to the Antichiesetta in the Ducal Palace, and from there to the Accademia. The stylistic similarity to Bonifazio de' Pitati, the painter of most of these votive pictures, and the freedom with which the traditional type of composition is treated and developed, are both remarkable. Mostra, Nos. 11 and 12.
Figs. 47, 48.

VENICE, ACCADEMIA

St. Louis, St. Jerome and St. Andrew. Originally in the Magistrato dei Governatori alle Entrate. In 1838 was transferred to the Academy of Fine Arts in Vienna and returned to Venice in 1919. The imitation of Bonifazio's Camerlenghi pictures is obvious and was noticed by Boschini (Minere 268). In the Vienna Academy the picture was attributed to Bonifazio and in the catalogue of the works sent back to Venice (1919, No. 22; G. Fiocco) it is described as "begun by Bonifazio and finished by Tintoretto." Pittaluga (p. 226) is inclined to assume some sort of collaboration and to anticipate by a few years the dating from 1557 given by G. Ludwig on the basis of the names of the donors, which appears convincing. On the other hand a double authorship must be rejected and the opinion of D. Westphal (Bonifazio Veronese, Munich 1931, p. 122) is correct : " In every stroke of the brush in this work, the gifted younger master can be recognized." Fig. 49.

VENICE, ACCADEMIA, No. 42

St. Mark rescuing a Slave. Signed : Jacopus tentor. f. From the Scuola Grande di San Marco, to which it was presented by the physician and philologist Tommaso Rangone. That it was finished in April 1548 is proved by a letter from Aretino to Tintoretto, in which he praises it warmly, but adds a warning against excessive haste and carelessness. An important work of the early period, and recognized as such by all authors from the beginning; in the seventeenth century Boschini styled it the most magnificent picture in the world, and in the nineteenth Taine considered it at least the most important picture in Italy (Thode, Repertorium XXIV, 11). On the other hand we know from Aretino's letters that it aroused opposition, and according to Ridolfi the members of the Scuola disliked it so much, that Tintoretto took it back and kept it for himself, until he was asked to hand it over. Mostra, No. 6. Figs. 21, 22.

VENICE, ACCADEMIA, No. 831

The Removal of St. Mark's Body. One of the series of scenes from the legend of St. Mark, begun in 1562, which Tintoretto painted at the behest of Tommaso Rangone for the Scuola Grande di San Marco. This picture has been considerably cut on the left, as can be seen from the engraving in Lovisa's Gran Teatro delle Pitture e Prospettive di Venezia, and from copies. The catalogue of the Mostra (No. 37) corrects the description of the scene as given by Ridolfi (and later by Bercken-Mayer), quoting the correct interpretation given by Borghini. The little picture in Brussels, supposed to be a sketch or model (see Hadeln, Jahrb. d. Preuss. Kunstsamml. XLII, p. 186) for the picture in Venice (Mostra, No. 36), seems to me to be a free variant by another hand after the finished picture. Fig. 113.

VENICE, ACCADEMIA, No. 832

The Miraculous Rescue of the Saracen by St. Mark. Of the same series as the preceding, and likewise cut down on the left. Mostra, No. 38. Figs. 110 and 111.

VENICE, ACCADEMIA, No. 875

Pax tibi Marce (The Dream of St. Mark). On December 28th, 1585, Tintoretto undertook to paint all the pictures still lacking in the hall of the Scuola di San Marco; in the following year they had not yet been begun, because the programme had not been settled. The other pictures of the series, which were later transferred to Santa Maria degli Angeli in Murano, were painted by Domenico. Our picture was likewise attributed to Domenico, until Mary Pittaluga (Bollet. d'Arte 1924, p. 33) produced strong grounds for returning it to Jacopo. The study of drawings connected with the painting (Tietze, Venetian Drawings, Nos. 1529, 1675) makes us, however, prefer the former attribution of this great painting to Domenico. Fig. 271.

VENICE, ACCADEMIA, No. 225

St. Justina with three Treasurers and their Secretaries. Signed with the date 1580 and the initials of the officials portrayed : Marco Giustinian, Angelo Morosini, Alessandro Badoer. Originally in the offices of the Camerlenghi at the Rialto and perhaps a companion-piece to the Berlin picture of 1569 (see above), the composition of which it develops. In bad state of preservation. Thode (Repertorium XXIV, 11) doubts that it is by Tintoretto's own hand, but Berenson, Osmaston, Bercken-Mayer and Pittaluga accept it. A drawing for this painting in Leningrad. (Tietze, Venetian Drawings, No. 1681.) Fig. 174.

VENICE, ACCADEMIA, No. 234

Portrait of the Procurator Andrea Cappello. From the Procuratie Nuove, but not mentioned by Boschini. Thode (Repertorium XXIV) was responsible for the not absolutely certain identification of the sitter, which would mean that the picture was painted about 1563, in which year Andrea Cappello, who died in the following year, became Procurator. Mostra, No. 40. Fig. 77.

VENICE ACCADEMIA, No. 236

Portrait of the Procurator Antonio Cappello. $43^{3/4} \times 31^{7/8}$. Inscribed : Antonius Cappello MDXXIII. From the Procuratie di Sopra, where Sansovino mentions the portrait without saying who painted it. Boschini attributed it to Titian. Of the modern writers Crowe and Cavalcaselle have suggested Damiano Mazza, while Thode (Repertorium, XXIV, p. 12 and Tintoretto, p. 80) was the first to propose Tintoretto, followed by all later writers, including the catalogue of the Mostra, No. 41. The catalogue also remarks that the date of the inscription refers to the year in which the Procurator, who died in 1564, took office. If we attempt to date it more exactly—which the catalogue does not try to do—we see clearly how difficult it is to fit the picture into Tintoretto's work. Neither the manner of the pose—with the expressive gesture of the articulated hand—nor the careful treatment of hair and skin are to be found in Tintoretto's other works.

VENICE, ACCADEMIA, No. 233

Portrait of Doge Alvise Mocenigo. From the Procuratie de Ultra. Can be dated from the sitter's period of office, 1570—1577. Mostra, No. 57. Fig. 158.

VENICE, ACCADEMIA, No. 237

Portrait of the Procurator Battista Morosini. Presented to the gallery in 1838 by the Contarini family. The sitter was identified by Thode (Repertorium, XXIV, 14) as Battista Morosini, born in 1537, who became Procurator in 1573. If this identification is correct, the picture must have been painted before 1573, probably shortly before. Mostra, No. 56.

VENICE, ACCADEMIA, No. 249

Portrait of Melchior Michiel. $24^{1/2} \times 19^{3/4}$. Inscribed : Melchior Michiel Eq. 1570. From the Procuratie de Sopra. One of eleven pictures painted for this office, for which Tintoretto was paid in 1571 (Hadeln, Jahrb. d. Preuss. Kunstsamml. 1911). The earlier attribution to Domenico is invalidated by his discovery, but I am not quite sure that the picture is by Tintoretto's own hand.

VENICE, ACCADEMIA

Portrait of Doge Girolamo Priuli. $39^{3/4} \times 33$. From the Procuratie de Ultra. Transferred to the Vienna Academy in 1838 and brought back to Venice in 1919. Priuli was Doge from 1559 to 1567, and payment was made for his portrait (Lorenzi, Documenti 307) on December 23rd, 1560. Our picture, which despite the bad state of preservation has good points, is generally recognized ; only Fiocco (Catalogo delle Opere d'Arte... 1919, 32) makes a few reservations.

VENICE, ACCADEMIA

Portrait of Ottavio Grimani. $43^{3/4} \times 42^{1/8}$. Inscribed : Octavs Grimanus, with the date 1560 and the Grimani arms. Transferred to the Academy in Vienna in 1838 and brought back to Venice in 1919. Formerly attributed to the school of Paris Bordone, but recognized as Tintoretto's in the Lützow catalogue of the Vienna Academy, No. 32, and in Fiocco's catalogue, op. cit., No. 95.

VENICE, CÀ D'ORO

Portrait of Nicolò Priuli. On the right, the Priuli arms. Originally in the Procuratie de Ultra, then in the repository of the Ducal Palace. Priuli became Procurator in 1545, and died in 1549, so that this portrait, sparkling with life, must have been painted between those years. Fig. 19.

VENICE, DUCAL PALACE, CEILING OF THE SALA DEGLI INQUISITORI

The Parable of the Prodigal Son. Octagonal.

Allegories of Faith, Justice, Strength and Charity. $26^{3/4} \times 80$. Mentioned by Borghini. Transferred to the Academy in 1817, and recently restored to their original position. They were part of the decoration destroyed by the fire of 1577, in which Tintoretto himself executed a large part of the work. The light and discreet colouring makes them particularly charming. A general sketch for the composition (Hadeln, Tintoretto's Drawings, Plate 13), fixing the positions of the chief figures, is discussed in Tietze, Venetian Drawings, No. 1648. Fig. 74.

VI*

VENICE, DUCAL PALACE, CEILING-PAINTING IN THE ATRIO QUADRATO

Doge Girolamo Priuli receiving the sword from Justice in the presence of St. Jerome and Venetia. Octagonal. Probably painted during Priuli's period of office (1559—1567), though Bercken-Mayer reduce the limits to 1561—1564. Pittaluga (p. 227) stresses the fact that the four putti in the corners, sometimes attributed to Tintoretto by older writers, and the four bronze-coloured Old Testament scenes at the sides of this ceiling are not by him. Fig. 90.

VENICE, DUCAL PALACE, CEILING-PAINTINGS IN THE SALA DELLE QUATTRO PORTE

Jupiter makes Venetia Queen of the Seas.

Venice as Defender of Liberty.

Juno presenting to Venice the Insignia of Power. Eight medallions with allegories of the cities and provinces under Venetian rule (Verona, Padua, Brescia, Istria, Treviso, Friuli, Vicenza, Altino; the last two, according to Ridolfi, II, p. 36, renovated by Francesco Ruschi). The general schema of the ceiling, created after the fire of 1574, was drawn up by Francesco Sansovino, who gives an exact description of it in his Venezia Città Nobilissima. Two compositions forming part of the scheme (Venice espousing Neptune and Venice leaning upon the World) were replaced in the eighteenth century by pictures by Tiepolo and Bambini. On the iconographic significance of this ceiling within the framework of the whole literary scheme for the redecoration of the Ducal Palace, see Konrad Escher, in Repertorium XLI, p. 93. That scarcely more than the general layout was done by Tintoretto himself was noticed by Thode (Repertorium XXIV, p. 27), who adds that even this limited participation is such as to excite our admiration of the sublime poetical motives. Bercken-Mayer (I, p. 77, 99) have done justice to the merits of the composition. Plate V (page 38).

VENICE, DUCAL PALACE, SALA DELL'ANTICOLLEGIO

Mercury and the Graces.

Bacchus and Ariadne

Minerva driving back Mars.

Vulcan and the Cyclopes. We learn from the entry regarding the payment to Tintoretto on November 10th, 1578 (he received fifty ducats for each picture, in accordance with the estimate made on July 26th, 1578, by Paolo Veronese and Palma Giovane), that the four pictures were intended to form an integral whole representing Concord; the allegorical references to Venice and the prudence of her administration are explained in detail by Ridolfi (II, pp. 43 ff). The pictures were painted for another room of the palace, the Salotto Dorato, but in 1716, when Bertuccio Contarini bequeathed to the Republic Paolo Veroneses's Rape of Europa and Jacopo Bassano's Return of Jacob to Canaan, they were transferred together with these to their present position. The high quality of composition has been specially emphasized by Bercken-Mayer. As to their criticism of the Vulcan's Smithy : "The figure seen from the back appears too predominantly sculptural in comparison with the other figures," it should be noted that this figure is derived from one in Signorello's Crowning of the Elect in Orvieto. Mostra, Nos. 59—62. Figs. 225—228, 230.

VENICE, DUCAL PALACE, SALA DEL COLLEGIO

Votive pictures of the Doges Andrea Gritti, Francesco Donato, Alvise Mocenigo, Nicolò da Ponte. These four pictures were painted in 1581—1584 to replace the corresponding paintings destroyed in the fire of 1577. At one time they were held to be by Tintoretto's own hand, and Thode was the first to dispute this theory (Repetorium XXIV, p. 28); he reduced the master's share to the designs. An idea of these in given by the large sketch for the Mocenigo picture in the Metropolitan Museum, New York (see above). The irregular manner in which the compositions of the destroyed pictures were followed in the substitutes is noticeable. In the votive picture of Gritti, most essential elements of Titian's composition have been retained, as is proved by a reproduction of the woodcut after it (in Tietze, Tizian, Plate XVIII and p. 134, ff., 311). Hadeln's thesis that the original votive painting for Donato, in the Sala del Collegio, had been painted by A. Schiavone, was rejected by Tietze, Venetian Drawings, p. 251. This composition is held by Pittaluga (L'Arte XXV, p. 86) to be the nearest to Tintoretto's own style in the whole group, whereas A. Venturi (Storia 9/IV, p. 659) assigns it to Domenico. In the other two votive pictures Tintoretto is less restrained; but, apart from the bad state of preservation, as is shown by a comparison with the sketch in New York, the large share taken by the workshop in the execution is a detriment to the quality. Bercken-Mayer (I, 228 f.) have

shown to what a great degree the compositions are developments on a large scale of the Virgin with the Chamberlains of 1567 (see above) and similar votive pictures. The spiritual content of the pictures has been investigated by Escher (Repertorium XLI, p. 96); they were painted not so much in a transcendental vein or with the idea of obtaining the help or protection of the Almighty, but rather with the firm conviction of being certain of divine help now and for ever.
Figs. 231—233, 235.

VENICE, DUCAL PALACE, SALA DEL SENATO, CEILING-PAINTING

Venice as Queen of the Seas. Executed by the workshop in 1581—1584 from a design by Tintoretto. Thode (Repertorium XXIV, p. 30) and Pittaluga (p. 229) ascribe the chief share to Domenico.
Fig. 229.

VENICE, DUCAL PALACE, SALA DEL SENATO

Votive pictures: Pietro Lando and Marcantonio Trevisan in prayer before the dead Christ. Pietro Loredan in prayer before the Virgin. Both pictures date from the period of the restoration of the Palace, 1581—1584. Thode (Tintoretto, p. 118, and Repertorium XXIV, p. 30) assumed for the former a derivation from an earlier picture painted by Tintoretto himself in 1554—1555 (Lorenzi, Monumenti, 608, 610, 614, 619), which was burnt in 1577; for the second, a decisive participation of Domenico. Pittaluga (p. 229) would sooner give the picture with the two Doges to Palma Giovane. In the picture of Loredan it seems to me that at least the conception must be Jacopo's.

VENICE, DUCAL PALACE, SALA DEL GRAN CONSIGLIO, CEILING-PAINTING

Triumph of Doge Nicolò da Ponte. This large painting is an atelier work, executed under Tintoretto's direction between 1580 and 1585. According to Ridolfi (II, p. 39) even Tintoretto's contemporaries criticized this picture after its unveiling as "fatte per prattica", in other words, mass production, an accusation which Tintoretto's pupils, Corona, Aliense and Francesco Crivelli, who had hidden themselves in the hall, energetically denied. Pittaluga (p. 231) is probably right in saying that these painters were most likely the very ones who had done most of the work on the picture. Drawings by Tintoretto for this ceiling listed in Tietze, Venetian Drawings, Nos. 1691, 1593, 1657, 1658.

VENICE, DUCAL PALACE, SALA DEL GRAN CONSIGLIO, CEILING-PAINTINGS

The Defence of Brescia.
The Battle near Riva.
The Battle of Argenta.
The Battle of Gallipoli. As they are mentioned by Borghini, they were probably executed shortly before 1584. Workshop paintings after designs by Tintoretto, who here allowed particularly fine conceptions to be executed by assistants.
Figs. 237, 238.

VENICE, DUCAL PALACE, SALA DEL GRAN CONSIGLIO

The Venetian Ambassadors before Frederick Barbarossa. Tintoretto contributed two pictures to the decoration of this hall as it was before the fire of 1577, the Excommunication of Barbarossa, painted in 1553, and his coronation as Emperor, 1562—1563. Hadeln gives these dates as probable in his contributions to the history of the Ducal Palace (Jahrb. d. Preuss. Kunstsamml. XXXII, Supplement), while in his notices on various pictures by Tintoretto (Amtliche Berichte XXXII, p. 163) he gives them as certain. The new picture, the contents of which are described fully by Bardi (G. Bardi, Dichiarazione di tutte le istorie... 1587, p. 139), was painted about 1584—1587. Thode (Repertorium XXIV, p. 25) doubted whether the execution was by Tintoretto's own hand. That the drawing in the Uffizi, No. 12954 (Hadeln, Tintoretto's Drawings, Plate 43), was used for a warrior in this picture is not—as Pittaluga (p. 231) assumes—in view of the customs of the workshop an argument in favour of Tintoretto's participation in the execution. The bad state of preservation of this much-restored picture adds to the poor effect in produces.
Fig. 240.

VENICE, DUCAL PALACE, SALA DEL GRAN CONSIGLIO

Paradise. The early history of this picture has been cleared up by Hadeln (Jahrb. d. Preuss. Kunstsamml. XL, p. 119), in amplification of Osmaston's investigations (The Paradise of T., 1910). It was painted after a competition held in 1579 for the redecoration of the hall after the fire of 1577 and in particular for the replacement of Guariento's Paradise painting which had been destroyed there. Of designs by other competitors we have one by Paolo Veronese in the museum at Lille, one by Francesco Bassano in the Hermitage and one by

Palma Giovane in the collection of Conte Contini, Florence, while Tintoretto's is now in the Louvre (see above). The painting was not executed at once; Bardi, who based his description of the restored palace on the programme, wrote in 1587 that Paolo Veronese and Francesco Bassano painted the Paradise. The painting, which was executed in the Scuola della Misericordia, must have been placed in position after that date. The differences from Tintoretto's design are explained by Hadeln—who notes the greater conformity of the finished painting with the other competing designs—as having been undertaken at the request of the authorities, who wanted a closer approximation to ecclesiastical tradition. The superiority of the sketch to the finished painting had already been noted by Algarotti and Goethe. This gigantic painting, the execution of which must certainly have been left entirely or for the greater part to the hands of pupils, suffered from a restoration carried out in the eighteenth century by Francesco Fontebasso, which is not the only restoration it has undergone. Nevertheless the general effect of the great composition, which, following the thirtieth canto of Dante's Paradiso, is based on the order of the Litany, is immeasurably great. A fragment with angels, which may have been near one of the doors, was reproduced by Soulier in Gazette des Beaux-Arts (1920, December); like the rest, it has the characteristics of an atelier work. The sketch in Madrid (see above), which some writers have connected with the Paradise, is only an imitation; the supposed sketch in Liverpool has nothing to do with our painting, the different format being sufficient reason for rejecting it. In the same way Josef Meder was mistaken in considering a number of pen-drawings · in the Studienbibliothek at Salzburg to be sketches and studies by Tintoretto for the Paradise; they are all by Palma Giovane and form part of the design which, as mentioned above, he submitted for the competition. (Tietze, Venetian Drawings, No. 1143.)
Folding plate, fig. 241, plate VI (page 55).

VENICE, DUCAL PALACE, SALA DELLO SCRUTINIO

The Battle of Zara. Painted in 1584—1587, attributed by contemporary writers (Bardi 139) to Tintoretto, by Zabeo (Elogio del T., 1813) to Andrea Vicentino; following Thode (Repertorium XXIV, p. 25), Pittaluga (Arte XXV, p. 91) would like to restrict Tintoretto's participation to the design, whereas Bercken-Mayer (I, p. 256, 270) expressly maintain that this powerful representation of a battle is undoubtedly a work of the master's. We know too little of the working methods in Tintoretto's atelier to be able to say exactly what the share of the master was. Several drawings now in the Uffizi were used for this work. (Tietze, Venetian Drawings, Nos. 1588, 1590, 1592, 1615, 1621.)
Fig. 236.

VENICE, LIBRERIA

Five Philosophers. Each picture about 92 × 54. The history of the decoration of Sansovino's Libreria has been expounded by Hadeln in his contributions to the study of Tintoretto (Jahrb. d. Preuss. Kunstsamml. XXXII, p. 25 ff., with an appendix thereto, XLII, p. 172). Whereas nothing now remains of the pictures which Tintoretto, together with a certain Domenico Molin of whom we know little else, painted in 1562 in the vestibule of the library ("after drawings, which shall be given him"), his Philosophers have been preserved and are now once more in their original position. The decoration was carried out in 1571—1572. Whereas Borghini attributed twelve philosophers to Tintoretto, later tradition recognized only four or five as his, while Osmaston and Thode (Repertorium XXIV, p. 17) even wanted to reject all but one. Nowadays the opinion prevails that five are by Tintoretto's own hand and one or two executed by the workshop, while the rest were painted by other artists, such as Paolo Veronese, Andrea Schiavone, etc. (Pittaluga, p. 236, where will also be found the complicated later history of the pictures, three of which went to Vienna in 1838 and returned to Venice in 1919, while others were damaged in 1902 when the Campanile collapsed). Bercken-Mayer (I, p. 143, 251) draw attention to the striking fact that the Philosophers, like the Prophets during the High Renaissance, are represented as simple men of the people. They mention also the deliberate contrast between the stately and sumptuous architecture and the poor clothing of the figures, a contrast which the Baroque period accentuated still more.
Figs. 160—164.

VENICE, FORMERLY IN SANT'ANNA

The Tiburtine Sibyl and Augustus. Mentioned and described by Borghini and Ridolfi, but not mentioned by Boschini or later writers. According to Thode (Repertorium XXIV, 440) probably removed from the church when it was reconstructed between 1634 and 1658. The hypothesis tentatively advanced by Thode, that this picture may be the same as that now in Palazzo Pitti (No. 257), which is attributed to Bordone or the workshop of Bonifazio, is rejected emphatically by Pittaluga in L'Arte XXIX, p. 38. It may, on the

contrary, be identical with a painting auctioned at the Ernst Museum, Budapest, in 1920, a very characteristic and wellpreserved work from the early 1550's.
Fig. 70.

VENICE, SAN CASSIANO

The Resurrection. Mentioned by Sansovino and Borghini, while Boschini states that it was signed. Thode (Repertorium XXIV, p. 426) remarks that the high altar was assigned to Tintoretto in accordance with a resolution taken January 1562 of the Scuola del Santissimo, and that the picture was executed in the 1565 under the guardian Zampiero Massoleggeri. This dating is confirmed by the style. The picture was restored in 1674 by Giuseppe Kalimper (who must be the German Josef Calimberg) and again later. It is in so bad a state of preservation that Ruskin's doubts as to its authenticity are comprehensible.

VENICE, SAN CASSIANO

Christ in Limbo. Painted in 1568 when the Guardian was Christino de' Gozi, who is certainly depicted as one of the donors on the right. The restoration in 1637, which had the reputation of being particularly bad, proved to be advantageous when the picture was displayed at the Mostra (No. 47). (For studies for the Christ and for Eve, s. Tietze, Venetian Drawings, Nos. 1558, 1620.)
Figs. 143, 147.

VENICE, SAN CASSIANO

The Crucifixion. It is generally assumed that this picture was painted at the same time as its pendant, the Christ in Limbo, i. e. in 1568. Mostra, No. 48.
Figs. 144, 145.

VENICE, SANTA CATERINA (at present in the Accademia)

Six scenes from the Legend of St. Catherine.
1. Disputation with the Emperor Maxentius.
2. The Saint being led away to martyrdom.
3. The attempt to break the Saint upon the wheel.
4. The Empress visits the Saint in prison.
5. Flagellation of the Saint.
6. Disputation with the Doctors of Alexandria.

Boschini assigns this cycle to the early period, but Ridolfi, more convincingly, to the late period. Pittaluga (p. 239) thinks that the latter dating is confirmed by the absence of the pictures from Borghini's list compiled in 1584. Whereas the conception of all the pictures may be attributed to Tintoretto, the hands of pupils can be detected in parts of the execution. Fiocco attributes No. 5 to Domenico, Nos. 1 and 6 to an artist whose painting was better than his drawing, perhaps Marco Robusti. Venturi (Storia 9/IV, p. 677) is reminded of the latter, of whom, it is true, no well established paintings are preserved. General reasons, however, seem to favour the attribution to Marco, as expounded in our Venetian Drawings, p. 294 f.
Fig. 280.

VENICE, SAN FELICE

St. Demetrius in armour. Coat-of-arms with the initials P G, which obviously denote a member of the Ghisi family. Berenson and Hadeln (Burl. Mag. 1922, II, p. 288) doubt its authenticity, but the state of preservation is so bad that it is impossible to form a definite judgement on this picture, which has been assigned by some to Tintoretto's earliest period. Thode (Repertorium, XXIV, p. 427) felt reminded of Bonifazio and Schiavone.

VENICE, SAN GALLO

Christ with Saints Mark and Gallus. In an unfavourable position and badly restored. Moschini (Guida di Venezia, 1815) speaks of rough cleaning, which Gasparo Diziani made good again (Thode, Repertorium XXIV, p. 428). Thode and others ascribe it to Tintoretto, but Hadeln rejects this (Burl. Mag. 1922, II, p. 288: follower of Bonifazio). It seems to me, however, to be more likely to be genuine than many other doubtful works of the early period.
Plate II (page 19).

VENICE, GESUITI

The Assumption. Mentioned by the contemporary authors, Sansovino and Borghini; Ridolfi states that the Crociferi, the predecessors of the Jesuits in this church, originally wanted to have the altar-piece painted by Paolo Veronese, but that Tintoretto succeeded in getting the contract by promising that he would paint in the style of Veronese; and in fact, by adapting his manner to that of Veronese he managed to achieve a very individual and magnificent result. Boschini describes the picture as "una delle singolari opere del mondo." Its influence on Baroque art (Carracci) has been noted by modern writers and especially by Bercken-Mayer. Unfortunately in the eighteenth century the picture was so extensively overpainted (Thode, Repertorium XXIV, p. 433), that it now reveals little of its once praised beauty; traces of it can be recognized in the composition, but a sort of eighteenth-century veil covers the whole. — Old copy in the Museum of Fine Arts, Boston.

VENICE, SAN GIORGIO MAGGIORE

The Gathering of Manna. Together with its companion-piece, the Last Supper, unanimously ascribed to the end of Tintoretto's life and activity, about 1594. The rich colouring of the picture was revealed for the first time after the recent cleaning. The subject, according to Thode (Tintoretto, p. 127) refers to Exodus xvi. 15: "This is the bread which the Lord hath given you to eat." The idea of the gift of daily bread and its spiritual connection with heavenly bread, administered in the companion piece (s. below), has been more fully dicussed by Dvořak, Italienische Kunst, II, 133 f.
Figs. 274, 264, 273, 262.

VENICE, SAN GIORGIO MAGGIORE

The Last Supper. Painted at the same time as the Gathering of Manna, the last and finest version of a theme so often treated by Tintoretto; the inevitable participation of assistants in so large a work does not detract from the effect. The supposed sketch in the museum at Boston, Mass. (No. 1532, cf. Ph. Hendy, Paintings by Tintoretto in Boston, in Burl. Mag. LXII, p. 129) seems to me more likely to be an XVIIIth century copy. Mostra, No. 73.
Figs. 275, 276, 277.

VENICE, SAN GIORGIO MAGGIORE

The Entombment. As the Chapel of the Dead, for which the picture was painted, was consecrated in 1592 and Tintoretto was paid seventy ducats for it in 1594, it must have been executed between those years. Thode's statement (Repertorium XXIV, p. 429) that it does not display Tintoretto's late style and must therefore have been painted earlier and then subsequently sold by him, is in contradiction with the universal belief that this is one of the master's very last pictures; the melancholy mood of the picture is explained by the catalogue of the Mostra (No. 74) as due to his grief at the death of Marietta in 1590. The unusually fine state of preservation of this late work is remarked upon by all.
Fig. 283.

VENICE, SAN GIORGIO MAGGIORE

Martyrdom of St. Stephen. The donation of the altar-piece was made on March 1st, 1593, so that the picture must belong to the very last period of Tintoretto's life; there is general agreement as to a considerable participation of the workshop. A general sketch for this altar-piece, at Christ Church, Oxford, has been attributed by Hadeln to Domenico, from which it would follow that the whole conception was due to the latter (Tintorettos Drawings, Plate 72). Adolfo Venturi (Storia 9/IV, p. 656) agrees with Hadeln and so did we in our Venetian Drawings, ad No. 1536. The grandiose conception of the San Giorgio picture and many of its details are so near to Jacopo that a supervision of this project by the still living old master seems likely.
Fig. 278.

VENICE, SAN GIORGIO MAGGIORE

Martyrdom of Saints Cosmas and Damian. Executed by the workshop in 1592—1593, from a design by Tintoretto.
Fig. 279.

VENICE, SAN GIORGIO MAGGIORE

The Resurrection, with St. Andrew recommending donors from the Morosini family. According to Thode (Repertorium XXIV, p. 429), painted between 1583 and 1588. Tintoretto's participation must be limited at most to the general design or drawings of single figures.

VENICE, SAN GIORGIO MAGGIORE

The Coronation of the Virgin. The altar-piece was commissioned on February 23rd, 1593, and the picture was paid for in 1594. To judge by the style, the chief share in the picture must be given to Domenico Tintoretto.

VENICE, SAN GIUSEPPE DI CASTELLO

St. Michael with a Senator as donor. Borghini, who mentions the picture in 1584, says that the donor was Michele Bon. The high quality of the picture is noted by Thode (Repertorium XXIV, p. 429), and its bad state of preservation by Pittaluga (p. 41). Both these authors and all others date it from the late period (Bercken-Mayer: Transition to the late works in San Rocco).
Fig. 269.

VENICE, SAN LAZZARO DEI MENDICANTI

St. Ursula. From the church of the Incurabili, where Sansovino and Borghini saw it. Came to San Lazzaro in 1817. A characteristic early work, about 1545. Mostra, No. 3.
Figs. 11, 12.

VENICE, SAN MARCO, MOSAICS

The large number of mosaics based on designs by Tintoretto and his son and executed from 1568 on by various mosaicists—G. A. Marini, Zuccato, Bart. Bozza, Domenico Bianchini, Lorenzo Ceccato—have been collected by Thode (Repertorium, XXIV, p. 430), on the basis of the material published by Pietro Saccardo (Les Mosaïques de St. Marc à Venise, 1896). Pittaluga (p. 242) has also dealt with this question. There are other documents to be found in Hadeln, Jahrb. d. Preuss. Kunstsamml., 1911, I.
Fig. 171.

VENICE, SAN MARCUOLA

The Last Supper. Inscribed: 1547 il 17 agosto in tempo di Miser Iseppo Morandello e compagni. On account of the exact dating and its being the earliest version of a theme so often painted by Tintoretto, this is an important work of the early period. When the church was rebuilt in the Baroque style (1728 to 1736) the picture was added to and overpainted (Gamba, Venezia, I), and it was not until the 1937 Mostra (catalogue, No. 2) that it was restored to its original format. The companion-piece, the Washing of Feet, is now in the Prado (see above) and there is a copy of it with similar additions still in San Marcuola.
Figs. 20, 13.

VENICE, SANTA MARIA DEL CARMINE

The Presentation in the Temple. A much discussed picture, assigned by Vasari to Schiavone, an attribution which Fröhlich-Bum (Jahrb. d. Kunsthistor. Sammlungen XXXI, 193) decisively rejects. Ridolfi gives it to Tintoretto; Hadeln (Burl. Mag. LII, 226) thinks it is neither by Schiavone nor by Tintoretto, but possibly by Jacopo Molino; Pittaluga (p. 225) suggests a pupil of Titian, perhaps Polid. Lanciano. On the other hand Bercken-Mayer (I, 53, 192), following Thode (Repertorium XXIV, 483), assign it definitely to Tintoretto, but with the reservation that it ought to be dated considerably earlier than 1548, the traditional date of its creation. It seems to me that there is much to be said for this view.
Plate II (page 19).

VENICE, SANTA MARIA MATER DOMINI

The Invention of the Cross. Whereas this picture, mentioned by Sansovino, is dated by Thode before 1545 (Repertorium XXIV, 434, and Tintoretto, p. 20), and by Bercken-Mayer, on account of the reminiscences of Parmeggianino, 1544—1547, Hadeln (Burl. Mag. 1922, II, 206), Pittaluga (p. 244) and, following her, the catalogue of the Mostra (No. 32), maintain that it cannot have been painted before 1561, the year in which the Scuola del SS. Sacramento, for which the picture was intended, was founded. Pittaluga would like to date it a trifle before 1561, but to me there seem to be no sound stylistic reasons for doing so.
Figs. 87, 85, 86.

VENICE, MADONNA DELL'ORTO

The Adoration of the Golden Calf

The Last Judgement. Mentioned as leading works by the contemporary writers, Vasari, Sansovino and Borghini. Ridolfi was the first to assign them definitely to the early period, and all other writers followed him until Thode (Repertorium XXIV, 432) who believed they were painted about 1560; Bercken-Mayer and Pittaluga accept this dating, while Soulier and Osmaston suggest 1546 and Berenson also says "early." All the stylistic features—above all the originality and monumentality of the invention—point rather to their

having been created in the mature period, about 1560. For the Adoration of the Golden Calf there was no tradition of an iconographic connection with the Last Judgement nor any compositional plan; Bercken-Mayer (I, 179) think it shows the preparations for the worship of the calf, in the same way as Baroque artists preferred to depict the preparations for a martyrdom, instead of the actual martyrdom. On the other hand, for the Last Judgement there was a tradition, which even Michelangelo followed. Tintoretto abandons frontality and achieves by means of an oblique arrangement of the scene a depth of space in which the prodigious event becomes a chaotic struggle, and not, as in other represent-ations of the subject, an orderly process of the other world. Reminiscences of Michelangelo's Last Judgement and of Titian's Gloria of 1554—among them the arrangement of the figures of the donors above on the right in the first layer of clouds—confirm the later dating. For the Golden Calf there are a few preparatory drawings. (See our Venetian Drawings, Nos. 1584, 1591, 1674.)
Figs. 91—94.

VENICE, MADONNA DELL'ORTO

The Presentation of the Virgin. Commissioned in 1551, Easter Sunday 1552 being the term fixed for delivery; the payments continued until 1556, but the picture had been finished before then (Mostra, No. 23). Vasari called it the best-executed work by Tintoretto in this church, and since then it has always been highly esteemed. For Thode (Tintoretto, p. 92) it was one of the greatest masterpieces in the world. The fantastic male figures standing or lying on the stairs to the left are interpreted by E. M. Phillipps as the representatives of different vocations, by Bercken-Mayer as the poor and infirm symbolizing the longing for the coming salvation, by Thode as representing the Old Testament in contrast to the brightly lighted women, who symbolize the New Testament.
Figs. 98—100.

VENICE, MADONNA DELL'ORTO

Four Angels bringing the Cross to St. Peter.

Martyrdom of St. Christopher. Originally the wings of an organ. Probably painted about 1560 like the two great pictures in the choir. Pendants—the earthly and the supernatural being contrasted, in each case, by marked contrasts even in the formal composition. In the Vision of St. Peter the divine phenomenon becomes a prodigy; in the Martyrdom, in its diminution, it becomes the aim and hope of the kneeling saint.
Figs. 95, 96.

VENICE, MADONNA DELL'ORTO

Five allegorical female figures (in the choir). Erroneously described by Borghini and Boschini as chiaroscuri, but actually executed with a certain amount of colour. In their present bad state of preservation they do not impress one as being by Tintoretto's own hand. Also painted about 1560.

VENICE, MADONNA DELL'ORTO

St. Agnes raising the Prefect's Son from the Dead. Mentioned by Vasari and Borghini, the latter adding that the donor was a Contarini. Thode (Repertorium XXIV, 435) identifies him as Tommaso Contarini, 1488—1578. Whereas most critics (and also the catalogue of the Mostra, No. 20), following Thode, date the picture early, Hadeln (Burl. Mag. 1922, II, 288) assigns it to the end of the 1560's, while Adolfo Venturi (Storia 9/IV, 684) dates it even later, assuming a considerable participation of Marietta. Both the colouring and the emphatic clarity of pose and movement seem to me evidence that it was painted very close to the first Miracle of St. Mark. Bercken-Mayer note that the figure falling head-downwards, a characteristic Tintorettesque invention, was used about 1555 by Titian in his picture of Perseus and Andromeda (Tietze, Titian, p. 230). The sketch in the Kaiser-Friedrich-Museum, Berlin (No. 1724), which Hadeln published as a preliminary study for this picture (Jahrb. d. Preuss. Kunstsamml. 1921, p. 186, and Amtliche Berichte XXXII, p. 163; cf. catalogue of the Mostra, No. 19), despite the similarity of the general arran-gement, shows such marked differences of composition and style that I am more inclined to think that it was a competing design by another hand (probably Schiavone's).
Figs. 27, 23, 24, 25.

VENICE, SANTA MARIA DEL ROSARIO (GESUITI)

The Crucifixion. Mentioned by Sansovino and Borghini, while the more recent writers unanimously date it from the 1550's, mostly between 1555 and 1560. Mostra, No. 26.

The distance from the quality of style achieved in the Last Supper in San Trovaso is considerable.

Fig. 50.

VENICE, SANTA MARIA DELLA SALUTE

The Marriage at Cana. Painted in 1561 for the Crociferi and mentioned as being there by Borghini in 1584; since 1657 it has been in the sacristy of the Salute. In its spatial construction and colouring it is one of the finest examples of Tintoretto's middle period (Mostra, No. 33). There is a smaller version, corresponding in every detail, in the Statens Museum at Copenhagen, No. 29, which is more likely to be a repetition than a sketch for the composition. A drawing for one of the servants in the Uffizi. Tietze, Venetian Drawings, No. 1634.

Fig. 116.

VENICE, SANTA MARIA ZOBENIGO

The Four Evangelists (on two panels). Begun in 1552, but, as demonstrated by Giul. Lorenzetti (Ateneo Veneto 1938, 3—4, p. 129 ff.), not finished until 1557. Originally used as wings for the organ, as Vasari states; Sansovino and Borghini also saw the pictures in this church (Mostra, Nos. 13 and 14). The pathetic seated postures of the Evangelists are derived from Central Italian mannerism.

Figs. 51—54.

VENICE, SAN MARZIALE

St. Marcelliano with St. Peter and St. Paul. According to payment entries, painted in 1549 and intended for the high altar, for the decorative accessories of which Tintoretto received several further payments in 1551 (Ludwig-Hadeln, Italienische Forschungen IV, 1911, p. 124). The derivation as to colouring from Titian's San Giovanni Elemosinario (Tietze, Titian, 132) is as evident as the relationship of the sitting figures with the pictures of saints painted in 1552 for the Magistrato del Sale (see above). Mostra, No. 9.

Fig. 26.

VENICE, SAN MOSÈ

The Washing of Feet. Mentioned by Sansovino, who does not give the subject, and then by Borghini, who does. Strips have been added above and below (Gamba, Venezia, I). The picture, which has grown dark with age and is difficult to see, is mostly assigned to the late period, but Mayer, who already in Bercken-Mayer (I, 206) had drawn attention to the importance of the composition, dates it in Burl. Mag. 1936, I, 281, very early, before 1553. that is to say about the same time as the Washing of Feet in the Escorial. One of his arguments in favour of this dating is that the pendant hanging opposite, the Last Supper ascribed to Palma Giovane, is not really by him, but is a late work of Bonifazio, who died in 1553. Neither in this nor in the other points does Mayer's line of argument seem to shake the general opinion. The composition is typical of the late period (e. g. The Last Supper in San Stefano), while the execution must be attributed for the most part to the workshop.

VENICE, SAN PIETRO IN CASTELLO

Paradise. Mosaic. Inscribed: Erminius Zucati 1570. Mentioned by Boschini as a work of Erminio Zuccato after a design by Tintoretto. This is accepted by the majority of scholars.

VENICE, SAN POLO

The Last Supper. Mentioned by Borghini in 1584; probably painted in the late 1560's. Thode (Repertorium XXIV, 437, and Tintoretto, p. 110) has drawn attention to the remarkable quality of this picture, which substitutes ecstatic emotion for the tranquil and peaceful atmosphere of earlier representations of the subject. Bercken-Mayer refer to the great admiration which contemporaries expressed for the picture, as is proved by the numerous copies and sketches made from it. Mostra, No. 49. A drawing for the landlord in the Victoria and Albert Museum. Tietze, Venetian Drawings, No. 1701.

Figs. 140, 115.

VENICE, REDENTORE

The Flagellation. According to Thode (Repertorium XXIV, p. 437), probably painted in 1592—1594, but completely disfigured by overpainting. Together with Pittaluga (p. 248) and Lorenzetti (Venezia e il suo Estuario, p. 723) I consider it a workshop production after designs by Tintoretto.

VENICE, REDENTORE

The Ascension, with numerous Saints. Like the preceding, probably painted in 1592—1594, and likewise much overpainted. That the execution is due to the workshop (Pittaluga and

Lorenzetti, op. cit.) seems certain, but Bercken-Mayer (I, p. 220) rightly drew attention to the originality and grandiosity of the composition, the conception of which must therefore in all probability be assigned to Tintoretto.

VENICE, SAN ROCCO

The Annunciation. Mentioned by Ridolfi (II, 18), together with the following picture, as wings of an organ. By the end of the eighteenth century, it had already been hung on the wall. Much restored, probably between 1574 and 1584. The unusual arrangement, in high, narrow format, with the scene in the open air, has been commented on by Bercken-Mayer (I, 189).
Fig. 167.

VENICE, SAN ROCCO

St. Roch before the Pope. See under the preceding picture.

VENICE, SAN ROCCO

The Pool of Bethesda. Painted in 1559 as the outside of a cupboard. Later—at all events before 1786—strips were added af the top and bottom, in order to make it symmetrical with Fumiani's Cleansing of the Temple. It was not until the 1937 Mostra that it was restored to its original form. Mentioned by Vasari; Ridolfi (II, 18) states that it was painted „in concorrenza col Pordenone." The adjustment of the style to Pordenone's St. Martin and St. Christopher, which hangs on the opposite wall, was an important factor in the creation of Tintoretto's picture, the relationship being clearly revealed by the excessively brilliant colouring and the overcrowding of the composition—with which Zanetti found fault. The picture, both for its dramatic power and the treatment of light, must be counted among Tintoretto's finest works. The way in which the two chief figures—the huge cripple carrying his bed and the Christ, who turns away to perform new miracles—press forward back to back, and the other sick people exhibit their pitiable bodies, is typical of Tintoretto's efforts to achieve the vision of the unreal by exaggerating the real. Mostra, No. 30.
Figs. 72, 71.

VENICE, SAN ROCCO

St. Roch visiting Sufferers from the Plague. In a document of 1565 we are told that Tintoretto had already painted in 1549 a picture for the choir chapel in the church of San Rocco; as the other pictures which he painted for this chapel in 1567 have been definitely identified, the one referred to must be our picture. This would agree with the fact that Vasari, who was in Venice in 1566, gives an exact description of it (".... with a very fine foreshortened corpse"). The style, however, does not fit in with the facts as set out in the catalogue of the Mostra, No. 45; for this reason Berliner (Kunstchronik 1919/20, 495) suggested that the date might be a clerical error for 1559. Is it possible that Tintoretto, when he began his new work for the church, revised his old picture? If we compare it with the Death of St. Roch, painted in 1567, we are inclined rather to regard the picture of the Plague as the later of the two. Bercken-Mayer (I, 241) say that this is the first hospital picture which inspired much imitation in the seventeenth century. In the manner in which a romantic atmosphere is created by means of a prison-like gloom shot with harsh lights, the influence of Titians's Martyrdom of St. Lawrence may perhaps be detected.
Figs. 135, 146.

VENICE, SAN ROCCO

St. Roch in Prison. In 1567 Tintoretto received payment for this and the following picture. Its completion—or at all events the end of his work on it—must be dated a little further back, as Vasari mentions it in that year with the words: "It is full of many beautiful and pleasing figures, and in short such that it is held to be one of the best works that this painter ever made." To judge by the vagueness of these words, Vasari, when he was in Venice in 1566, cannot have seen it, or at all events not when it was completed. The picture shows the saint imprisoned by order of his father, the Prefect of Antioch, either at the moment of his entering the prison or at that of his death (Bercken-Mayer, I, 241). The same authors note the gruesome element (the head lying on the grating) and other figures, which are probably derived from the engraving (B. XV, p. 412, 66) after Giulio Romano. Mostra, No. 46.
Figs. 136, 138.

VENICE, SAN ROCCO

St. Roch healing the Animals. Painted in 1567 together with the preceding picture, but unlike the latter, mainly a workshop production.

VENICE, SAN ROCCO

St. Roch taken prisoner. Pittaluga (p. 249) dates this workshop picture between 1577 and 1584; but it may have been painted shortly after 1567 just after the other paintings for the choir. A large autograph sketch at Colnaghi's, London in 1946/47, Fig. 286, s. above.

VENICE, SAN SEBASTIANO

The Adoration of the Brazen Serpent. Although this painting, which forms part of the decoration of the sacristy, was attributed by Vasari and Sansovino to Tintoretto, its authenticity has continually been doubted, for it shows none of his characteristic features. That it was painted, as Vasari says in explanation of its unusual nature, "in competition with Paolo Veronese" appears improbable for chronological reasons; I should be more inclined to suggest a casual collaboration of Tintoretto with Bonifazio's workshop, which was entrusted with the decoration of the sacristy walls. In any case Tintoretto's participation in the painting of this much deteriorated work remains somewhat problematical.

VENICE, SAN SILVESTRO

The Baptism of Christ. Mentioned in 1584 by Borghini. In 1838, in order to adapt it to a new altar, it was enlarged on all four sides and revised. It was not until the 1937 Mostra that it was freed from these additions. An important late work, probably painted about 1580 or very shortly afterwards. The Uffizi possesses drawings (12943 and 12961) for the two figures (Tietze, Venetian Drawings, Nos. 1598, 1609). The sharpness of the silhouette effects, together with the very tender and moving sensibility, may be due to a renewal of Titianesque inspiration, such as may be seen in Tintoretto's works just after Titian's death.
Fig. 270.

VENICE, SAN SIMEONE GRANDE

The Last Supper. Mentioned by Borghini. Owing to the bad state of preservation and the unfavourable location, it is difficult to form an opinion (Pittaluga, p. 257). The conception, which lies between the pictures in San Trovaso and San Polo, might in view of the rationalization of the treatment of space (Marriage at Cana, later Miracles of St. Mark) belong to the beginning of the 1560's. Though beautiful in parts, especially in the left half of the picture, it is difficult to ascribe the mediocrity of the right half entirely to clumsy restoration. We must assume collaboration of assistants.

VENICE, SANTO STEFANO

The Agony in the Garden. Originally in Santa Margarita, where Sansovino and Borghini saw it. A late work, about 1580, closely related to the contemporary representation of the same subject in the Scuola di San Rocco. Mostra, No. 69. A drawing for one of the apostles in the Victoria and Albert Museum. (Tietze, Venetian Drawings, No. 1697.)
Figs. 266, 265.

VENICE, SANTO STEFANO

The Washing of Feet. See the preceding picture, with which it is stylistically related. A drawing in the Uffizi contains studies for the principal group of this picture. (Tietze, l. c., No. 1632.)
Fig. 267.

VENICE, SANTO STEFANO

The Last Supper. Belongs with the two other pictures in San Stefano as regards origin and style. Compared with the other great late versions of this theme, it produces a rather cool effect and not all of it is by Tintoretto's own hand (Mostra, No. 68).
Fig. 178.

VENICE, SAN TROVASO

The Last Supper. Mentioned by Borghini and engraved by E. Sadeler. An important work, about 1560. Mostra, No. 27. Three studies from a clothed model, in a drawing in Berlin, are used in this painting. (Tietze, Venetian Drawings, No. 1563.)
Figs. 88, 114.

VENICE, SAN TROVASO

The Adoration of the Magi. Mentioned by Ridolfi as a work of Tintoretto's last years, then in the church of Santa Maria Maggiore, which has since been demolished. Martinioni (Venezia, con l'aggiunta di tutte le cose... 1663, p. 269) ascribes it to Domenico Tintoretto, whose participation Pittaluga (p. 258) rightly describes as obvious. The general conception was Jacopo Tintoretto's.
Fig. 281.

VENICE, SAN TROVASO

The Expulsion of Joachim from the Temple. Originally with the preceding picture and the
Nuptials of the Virgin in the parish church at Riese (see above). A typical workshop
picture, in which Pittaluga (p. 258) discerns the participation of another hand than
Domenico's.
Fig. 282.

VENICE, SAN TROVASO

The Temptation of St. Anthony. Probably painted in 1577 to the order of Antonio Mille-
donne, secretary to the Senate, and first mentioned by Borghini in 1584. The dating is
supported by the close stylistical resemblances to the mythological paintings of 1577 in
the Anticollegio at the Ducal Palace. Mostra, No. 58.
Fig. 176.

VENICE, SAN ZACCARIA

Nativity of John the Baptist. First mentioned by Sansovino and Borghini. An early work,
akin to the Visitation at Bologna. In the general conception, reminiscences of Dürer's
woodcut of the Nativity of the Virgin (B. 80) are perceptible, and in the large hovering
angels, which also occur in other early works, perhaps the influence of the Dutch
mannerists. On the enlarged version of the composition in the Hermitage at Leningrad,
see above.
Fig. 4.

VENICE, SCUOLA DI SAN ROCCO

Ceiling-paintings in the Sala dell'Albergo. Central compartment : St. Roch in Glory. In the
four corners, heads of Seraphim; in the lateral compartments, allegories of the other
" Scuole Grandi" in Venice, of the Virtues and Seasons. Beneath the ceiling, a frieze of
putti with flowers and fruits; between the windows, in simulated niches, two Prophets.
The decision to promote a competition among three or four of the best Venetian painters
for a picture for the oval central compartment was formulated by the principals of the
Brotherhood of San Rocco on May 21st and 31st, 1564. Simultaneously subscriptions were
raised for the purpose from the members of the Brotherhood, most of whom contributed
from two to fifteen ducats. Messer Zammaria de' Zigninnoni dalla Sede promised fifteen
ducats on condition that the painting should not be executed by Tintoretto, but by
another; if the work were to be given to Tintoretto, he would give nothing. It is thus
evident that Tintoretto's name had already been suggested. Ridolfi gives a detailed
description of how he stole a march on the other competitors by submitting, instead of
designs as the others did, the finished picture, and even smuggled it into position. Ridolfi's
further statement that Tintoretto made a present to the Brotherhood of the picture he had
thus imposed upon them, is confirmed by the protocol of July 22nd, 1564, which announces
the formal acceptance of the gift. Some of the members, among them probably the above-
mentioned adversary of Tintoretto, were not satisfied with this solution and wanted to
remove the smuggled picture from the place of honour in the middle of the ceiling. When
the competition announced on May 31st was annulled as superfluous, thus giving official
approval to Tintoretto's trick, twenty members opposed the motion, as against thirty-one
who voted for it.—The remaining ceiling-paintings and the rest of the decoration of the
Albergo were completed in 1566-67 (Rudolf Berliner, Die Tätigkeit Tintorettos in der
Scuola di San Rocco, Kunstchronik 1919-20, p. 68 ff.; and Rodolfo Pallucchini, Tintoretto
a San Rocco, 1937, p. 8 ff.). There are five drawings connected with the allegorical ceiling-
paintings (Tietze, Venetian Drawings, Nos. 1565, 1586, 1597, 1613, 1631). The frieze of putti
is very faded, but in 1905 a covered portion of it was discovered which had been protected
from the light and had preserved a surprising freshness of colour. In his " Théories" Maurice
Denis warns us against drawing conclusions from this fragment as to the original colouring of
Tintoretto's pictures, as it is only a grounding, which would have toned after being worked
over with umber.
Figs. 122, 120, 121.

VENICE, SCUOLA DI SAN ROCCO, SALA DELL'ALBERGO

The Crucifixion. Inscribed : MDLXV—Tempore Magnifici Hieronimi Rotae et Collegarum
Jacobus Tintorectus facebat. On the back of the picture there are marks from which we
can deduce that the figures were first painted in the nude and then clothed in draperies
(Pittaluga, L'Arte 1921, p. 202). One of the chief works, praised by Vasari and by all later
writers, and often engraved—for the first time by Agostino Carracci in 1589. The most
concise praise of the work was formulated by Ruskin, who in his eloquent description of all
the pictures in San Rocco in Stones of Venice III, 379, when he comes to the Crucifixion
breaks off with the words : "I must leave this picture to work its will on the spectator,

for it is beyond all analysis, and above all praise." The essential elements in this magnificent composition are the homogeneous concentration of scene and action by means of light, the clear articulation of the spatial area by means of the two chief diagonals intersecting at the Cross, the raising of the crucified Christ, conceived as clear vertical and horizontal lines, above the tumult of the spectators, and the contrast between the lonely death and the bustling indifference of the crowd, of whom only the group at the foot of the Cross take a sympathetic interest in what is happening. The breach of tradition, in that the Virgin, instead of standing beneath the Cross, has sunk to the ground, has been frequently denounced by defenders of ecclesiastical orthodoxy. Several preliminary drawings for single figures have been preserved (s. Tietze, Venetian Drawings, Nos. 1585, 1664, 1702, 1594, 1710). Various other drawings and pictures held to be preliminary studies for this composition—among them the Crucifixion in Schleissheim (No. 997) of which Thode and Bercken-Mayer have far too high an opinion—are copies or otherwise derived from the picture in San Rocco (Pittaluga, p. 250). The painting in Schleissheim, originally in the Augustiner Church in Munich, was executed in 1585 for Herr Sebastian Füll, of Munich, and engraved by J. Jenner in 1623. (R. A. Peltzer, in Alte Kunstschätze aus Bayern, 1934, p. 63). Folding plate, Figs. 127—132, 134.

VENICE, SCUOLA DI SAN ROCCO, SALA DELL'ALBERGO

Christ before Pilate.
Ecce Homo

Christ bearing the Cross. The execution of these scenes from the Passion dates from the years 1566 and 1567. They fill the wall opposite the Crucifixion, the restricted space above the door being used for the Ecce Homo, while the two great figures flanking it form a transition to the two neighbouring compositions. In the Christ before Pilate, the chief emphasis is laid on the contrast between the brightly lighted pillar-like figure of Christ with its whitish-grey draperies, which the vertical lines of the architecture in the background set off still more, and the other restlessly moving figures, overlapping and overlapped, which shade off into various tones of darkness or semidarkness. Perhaps Dürer's woodcut of the Passion (B. 32) provided some inspiration for this. The chief motif of "Christ bearing the Cross" is the anxious to-and-fro movement of the procession, the contrast between the bright silhouettes standing out against the hill in the foreground and the dark figures against the bright sky in the background, and the placing of the chief figure back in the middle distance. (A Crucifixion from the von Sierstorff collection, shown in the exhibition of pictures loaned from German private collections at Frankfort, 214, Plate XXXIV of the catalogue, said to be a late work by Tintoretto and discussed in Cicerone 1925/II, 734, seems to me, as far as one can judge without having seen the original, to be a typical workshop variant of the composition in San Rocco.) Whereas in the scene before Pilate Christ appears as the heroic counterpart of all the dark powers, in the second picture he is the tiny helpless victim of an overpowering destiny. There is a drawing for one of the thieves in the Uffizi (No. 13028, our Venetian Drawings, No. 1640). Figs. 123—126.

VENICE, SCUOLA DI SAN ROCCO, UPPER HALL

Ceiling-Paintings.

1. Adam and Eve.
2. Moses bringing forth water from the Rock. $218^{1}/_{2} \times 206^{3}/_{4}$.
3. The Vision of Moses. $147^{1}/_{4} \times 104$.
4. The Pillar of Fire in the Wilderness. $147^{1}/_{4} \times 104$.
5. The Brazen Serpent. $329 \times 206^{3}/_{4}$.
6. The Salvation of Jonah. $104 \times 147^{1}/_{4}$.
7. The Sacrifice of Isaac. $104 \times 147^{1}/_{4}$.
8. The Vision of Ezekiel. $259^{1}/_{4} \times 104$.
9. Jacob's Ladder. $259^{1}/_{4} \times 104$.
10. The Gathering of Manna. $218^{1}/_{2} \times 206^{3}/_{4}$.
11. Elisha multiplying the Loaves. $147^{1}/_{4} \times 104$.
12. Elijah receiving food from the Angel. $147^{1}/_{4} \times 104$.
13. The Paschal Feast.

Work began on these ceiling-paintings in 1575-76 with the middle picture (The Brazen Serpent), was continued in 1577 with the two other miracles of Moses (2 and 10), and was finished by 1581, together with the general decoration of the hall. In the eighteenth century the pictures were in such a bad state of preservation that in 1741 a restoration was planned, which, as the protocol of the Scuola concerning it states, was limited to a mere cleaning, all overpainting being avoided. In 1777 the matter again came to notice. In an expert report, Antonio Maria Zanetti proposed that the restorer should be Giuseppe Angeli and recommended the removal of eighteen deteriorated pictures from the ceiling and their replacement by copies. This was not carried out, but in 1778 the pictures were restored and new-lined by Angeli, with less rigorous restrictions than in 1741 (R. Bratti, Un mancato sostituto del Tintoretto nel Secolo XVIII, Rivista della Città di Venezia 1927, p. 31). The small rectangular compartments were rendered unrecognizable.

The iconographic programme of the whole Upper Hall has been dealt with in particular detail by Thode (Repertorium XXVII, p. 34). It links up the usual typological system of the late Middle Ages, which connected the events of the Old Testament with those of the New, of which they were the prophecies, and the charitable mission of the Brotherhood (quenching the thirst of the thirsty, healing the sick, feeding the hungry); the three chief pictures refer to these subjects (Moses bringing forth water from the Rock, the Brazen Serpent, the Gathering of Manna). Kindred representations are grouped round each of these, while the corresponding wall-pictures rise from the alleviation of bodily needs to the satisfying of spiritual necessities.

We thus get the following arrangement:

Introduction: The Fall of Man (1); Wall-pictures, The Nativity and Temptation.

First Group: Moses bringing forth Water from the Rock, Vision of Moses, Pillar of Fire, Salvation of Jonah (2, 3, 4 & 6); wall-pictures, Baptism of Christ and the Pool of Bethesda.

Second Group: The Brazen Serpent, Vision of Ezekiel, Jacob's Ladder, Sacrifice of Isaac (5, 7, 8 & 9); wall-pictures, Resurrection and Ascension, Raising of Lazarus and Agony in the Garden.

Third Group: Gathering of Manna, Elisha multiplying the Loaves, Elijah fed by the Angel, the Paschal Feast (10, 11, 12 & 13); wall-pictures, Feeding of the Five Thousand and Last Supper.

Beneath the Paschal stands the altar. "Once again the sacred subjects of the Middle Ages and the Renaissance achieve new life in the fantasy of a great master" (Thode). The pictures are painted with a view to their being placed in a high position. The three compositions with many figures correspond to the construction of the walls; the others, which are limited to single figures, show these disproportionately large, which on the one hand gives an effect of directness and nearness of vision, and on the other hand gives additional energy to the crowded compartments.

Figs. 186—198.

VENICE, SCUOLA DI SAN ROCCO, UPPER HALL

Ten wall-paintings of scenes from the Life of Christ.

1. The Nativity.
2. The Baptism.
3. The Temptation.
4. The Raising of Lazarus.
5. The Pool of Bethesda.
6. The Miracle of the Loaves and Fishes.
7. The Agony in the Garden.
8. The Last Supper.
9. The Resurrection.
10. The Ascension.

The pictures were painted from 1576 to 1581. They complete the typological system of the ceiling decoration, with the spatial arrangement of which they also correspond (see above). As regards composition, the pictures hung opposite each other form in each case a pair (see p. 43). Detailed analyses of these paintings will be found in Thode, Tintoretto, p. 99 ff., and Pallucchini, op. cit., 67 ff. It should be noted that no preliminary sketches for these paintings have been preserved; that mentioned by Thode, op. cit., 110, for the Pool of Bethesda, in the Holford collection, London, is not accepted by Osmaston; the so-called sketch for the Last Supper in the Academia de San Fernando, Madrid (Osmaston II, 123), has been identified by Christopher Norris as a copy—mentioned by Palomino—by Velázquez, reproduced in Burl. Mag. 60, 157. Of drawings for single figures a few have been preserved, s. Tietze, Venetian Drawings, Nos. 1653, 1704, 1712, 1758. Figs. 200—209, 212, 214—218.

VENICE, SCUOLA DI SAN ROCCO, UPPER HALL

The Vision of St. Roch. An altar-piece. Painted in 1588. Darkened and deteriorated, which may partly explain the unfavourable effect it produces. In the execution of the painting Tintoretto's shop had a large part.

Fig. 199.

VENICE, SCUOLA DI SAN ROCCO, UPPER HALL

St. Roch—St. Sebastian. On the window wall opposite the altar, painted during the period of work which began in 1576. Pallucchini, p. 67, draws attention to the fact that Greco, who went to Spain in this year, follows Tintoretto's model in the signed Sebastian in Valencia Cathedral, from which we may perhaps conclude that he had seen a drawing or a preliminary study. The fact does not help us to date either of the pictures more exactly. The movement in these pictures is as bold as that in any of the artist's works; the tranquillity of the usual representations of sacred figures is replaced by passionate emotion.
Figs. 210, 211.

VENICE, SCUOLA DI SAN ROCCO, UPPER HALL

So-called Self-portrait. Inscribed : Religio(ni?) 1573. There is no old tradition to support the description of this picture as a self-portrait. Hadeln, who recognized it as a work by Tintoretto, held that it was the portrait of some functionary of the Scuola. Pallucchini has recently tried to decipher the character of the artist from this physiognomy (op. cit., p. 85). But it is difficult to find any resemblance to the best-authenticated self-portrait in the Louvre.
Fig. 179.

VENICE, SCUOLA DI SAN ROCCO, STAIRCASE

Visitation. 63 × 94¹/₂. A late work from the 1580's. Mostra, No. 65.
Figs. 263, 257.

VENICE, SCUOLA DI SAN ROCCO, GROUND-FLOOR

Annunciation. Painted between 1583 and 1587. The combination of splendour and intimacy— the subject-matter has been interpreted by Thode (Tintoretto, p. 102)—gives this picture a place between Italian and Northern painting. Soulier's comparison with Dürer's woodcut of the Adoration, B 85, is rejected by Pallucchini (op. cit., p. 87), who would probably have rejected even more emphatically Th. Hetzer's comparison with Altdorfer's Nativity in Munich (Das Deutsche Element in der italienischen Malerei des 16. Jahrhunderts, Berlin 1929, p. 138). Although a direct connection with the woodcut or picture is actually improbable, there is some justification for the comparisons. The extension of the tangible proximity—emphasized in its tangibility—into endless space came to Tintoretto from Northern art, and the influence of the later art production, saturated with Dürer and the Danube style, may have been helped by the presence in his atelier of Dutch assistants. The Italian monumentality of the principal group forms an all the more curious contrast to this so different conception of space.
Figs. 246, 255.

VENICE, SCUOLA DI SAN ROCCO, GROUND-FLOOR

Adoration of the Magi. Painted between 1583 and 1587. Thode (Tintoretto, p. 102) rightly draws attention to the bad state of preservation. The composition of light and shadow is dramatic, and Boschini aptly defined it as "un gran concerto." The complicated architectural construction is intended only to motivate and regulate the play of light and to render possible a free disposition of the figures. The ghostly procession of the retinue of the Magi in the right background is fantastic.
Figs. 248, 251, 254.

VENICE, SCUOLA DI SAN ROCCO, GROUND-FLOOR

The Flight into Egypt. Painted between 1583 and 1587. As with the Annunciation, one might be attempted to detect Northern influences (Dürer) in this picture—in the proportions of the principal group of figures to the landscape, in the repoussoir motif of the wicker fence on the right ; of paramount importance, however, is the fact, emphasized by Thode (Tintoretto, p. 103) and recently by Pallucchini (p. 21), that the picture follows the Venetian tradition, the lyricism of which here rises to heights of splendour. The rich colouring of the Virgin shows the influence of Titian's Assunta period, the house on the water behind on the right that of Titian in his Giorgionesque period, or of Giorgione himself. All naturalistic elements are fused in the free play of fantasy. According to Thode it is—despite Rembrandt—the finest landscape ever painted.
Figs. 247, 252, 272.

VENICE, SCUOLA DI SAN ROCCO, GROUND-FLOOR

The Massacre of the Innocents. Painted between 1583 and 1587. This composition owes something to Giovanni da Bologna's Rape of the Sabines (E. Tietze-Conrat, Graph. Künste, new series I, p. 89) and also to Raphael's Burning of the Borgo. Something of the general

violence of these models is noticeable in that the actual event is not clearly shown; "he conceals the children and the weapons in the hands of the murderers and shows only men and women struggling" (Thode, Tintoretto, p. 104). The scene is thus more of an orgy of passion than a historical narrative; the boldness of the brushwork, especially in the episodes in the background, explains why Pallucchini (op. cit., p. 99) mentions the name of Delacroix in connection with this picture.
Figs. 258, 250, 253, 256.

VENICE, SCUOLA DI SAN ROCCO, GROUND-FLOOR

The Presentation in the Temple. Painted between 1583 and 1587. Somewhat more antiquated in style than the other pictures in this room, of which the Adoration of the Magi is the most akin to it; but a comparison of the two shows that the Presentation in parts has defects which must be attributed to a considerable participation of the workshop. A signed and dated drawing by Rottenhammer in the National Gallery of Scotland at Edinburgh show small discrepancies probably due to restoration; the drawing is a proof of the studies undertaken by Rottenhammer in the Scuola, as stated in the older writers.
Fig. 249.

VENICE, SCUOLA DI SAN ROCCO, GROUND-FLOOR

The Assumption. Long and conspicuous inscription added during restoration. Painted between 1583 and 1587. The format, unusually broad for this subject, was necessary for the original conception—the Virgin ascending to Heaven in the midst of the Apostles. The execution was badly injured by Antonio Florian's restoration in 1784; of this Ruskin remarked: "The man to whom the task was committed providentially died, and only one of the paintings was spoiled."
Fig. 259.

VENICE, SCUOLA DI SAN ROCCO, GROUND-FLOOR

St. Mary Magdalen.

St. Mary Aegyptiaca. Painted between 1583 and 1587. Masterpieces of the late style. Pallucchini (op. cit., p. 103) notes that the old descriptions of the Scuola, some of them so detailed, make no mention of these pictures. The landscape dominates with its nocturnal mystery and glittering moonlight, and with its solemn atmosphere envelops the little figures of the meditating Saints, who abandon themselves to the contemplation of eternity without heeding the spectator. The colouring has become a conveyor of mood, the farewell mood of the grey-haired master.
Figs. 260, 261.

VENICE, ITALICO BRASS COLLECTION

Venus pursued by Minerva. 75¼ × 91. Bercken, who reproduced the picture in Pantheon 1935, I, p. 24, assigns it to the late period and describes it as the better version of the composition, there being a school version in the Prado.

VICENZA, PINACOTECA, No. 74

St. Augustine healing forty cripples. 61 × 67. Originally in the church of San Michele, Vicenza, where Ridolfi (II, 49) and Baldinucci (VI, 376) mention a painting of this subject. Soulier's suggestion (Tintoretto, p. 88) that the picture now in the Uffizi (No. 914) is the one from San Michele, is rejected by Pittaluga (p. 287), on the grounds that the Uffizi picture is a copy by Domenico. Pittaluga defends the Vicenza picture, described by Thode (Tintoretto, p. 124) as a ruin, against the doubts expressed by Osmaston (II, 212) as to its authenticity. Still more emphatically is it claimed for Jacopo Tintoretto's early period (1549-50), and as one of his masterworks to boot, by R. Pallucchini in his catalogue of "I capolavori dei Musei Veneti," Venice 1946, No. 231. The subjectmatter was reinterpreted by U. Middeldorf in The Art Bulletin, 1944, p. 195.

VIENNA, GEMÄLDEGALERIE

No. 159. *The Feast of Belshazzar.*
No. 175. *The Queen of Sheba before Solomon.*
No. 184. *David bringing back the Ark of the Covenant.*
No. 195. *The Promise to David.*
No. 184a. *The Prostration of Bathsheba.*
No. 203. *The Vengeance of Samson.*

All painted on pine-wood. The homogeneity of this series of six Old Testament scenes, originally intended for the adornment of furniture, is generally accepted with certain reservation. Whereas the 1907 guide to the gallery ascribed all six pictures to Schiavone, L. Fröhlich-Bum (Jahrb. d. Kunsthist. Samml. XXXI) gave only Nos. 184 and 203 to Schiavone and held that the others were painted in Bonifazio's workshop. Hadeln (Zeitschrift f. Bild. Kunst 1922, p. 29) claimed that the whole series was by Tintoretto, though he admitted the participation of another hand in Nos. 159 and 175; his attribution has been accepted in the main by later writers (Berenson, Bercken-Mayer, Pittaluga), and also his dating from the early period, shortly before 1548. There is external confirmation of this in Ridolfi's statement (II, 15) that in his youth Tintoretto painted cassoni, which he exhibited under the Procuratie with other painters.

Although Hadeln's attribution is on the whole convincing, it is not quite safe to assert that the whole series was originally conceived as a homogeneous group. The sameness of technique and format may be explained by the fact that we have here to do with typical products. Stylistically the pictures seem to go in pairs, which would be the case if they were used for cassoni. The comparisons between the three pairs are based on the uniformity of format and execution of all pictures in Tintoretto's early workshop. In Nos. 159 and 175, for which Hadeln admitted the participation of another hand, the relationship to Bonifazio is evident, the light cheerful colouring agreeing with the clear narration delighting in charming details. It is characteristic that the other pictures are more obscure and less easy to interpret (cf. E. Tietze-Conrat, Kunstchronik 1922, p. 33 ff.). The figures are more robust, the colouring more subdued, the whole execution broader and more sketchy, and the conception more dramatic. The representation of Samson's vengeance and Bathsheba's prostration differs fundamentally from the fairy-tale atmosphere of the pair first mentioned. Between these two pairs we have Nos. 184 and 195, closely akin to each other in colouring and treatment of space. The differences between the three pairs—which, however, have certain points of contact (cf., for example, the two men gazing into the distance on the extreme left of No. 184a with the almost identical group beneath the arboured walk in No. 175)—could be explained as due to different dates of execution and the collaboration of different assistants. An idea of the way the workshop functioned is provided by the sketch for the Queen of Sheba in the museum at Aachen, where the elements in the left half of the Vienna picture are grouped quite differently. These pictures for furniture must have been frequently undertaken by the workshop from the beginning. Nos. 159 and 175 may have been painted about 1545, the others about 1548, since—apart from the format—they have already achieved the same level of style as the first Miracle of St. Mark. As to the question of collaborators, it is well to bear in mind the trustworthy tradition according to which Lambert Sustris, before he left Venice in 1560, worked in Tintoretto's atelier as a painter of landscapes; especially in the landscape of No. 184 we can perceive traces of Northern conception and a certain similarity with the earlier works of Sustris, e. g. the Baptism of Christ at Caën (Jahrb. d. Kunsthist. Samml. in Wien XXXI, Plate XXVII). The question of Tintoretto's cassoni, including the four pictures in the Museo Civico at Verona which Hadeln holds to be copies (reproduced by L. Fröhlich-Bum, ibid., p. 191 f.), still needs thorough investigation.
Figs. 32—39, 42—46.

VIENNA, GEMÄLDEGALERIE, No. 239

Susanna bathing. Probably the picture mentioned by Ridolfi as belonging to the painter Nicolò Renier in Venice in 1648; in Vienna since 1824. Variously dated between the 1550's (Bercken-Mayer) and about 1570 (Pittaluga); the catalogue of the Mostra (No. 34) follows the dating given by the Vienna gallery, shortly after 1560. There is complete unanimity as to the exceptionally high artistic merit of this picture.
Colour plate, Figs. 61, 62.

VIENNA, GEMÄLDEGALERIE, No. 254a

The Flagellation. Has been cut down at the bottom and on the left. Purchased in 1923 from the art market. Hadeln, who was the first to publish it (Burl. Mag. XLVIII, p. 115), notes the resemblance of the figure of Christ to a terracotta relief by Giambologna in the Kaiser-Friedrich-Museum, Berlin, and considers this a confirmation of Borghini's statement that Tintoretto in his late period made studies after the sculptures of Giambologna. A drawing in the Uffizi (Our Venetian Drawings No. 1603) seems to form a link between the relief and the painting. The drawing offers close relationship to Domenico Tintoretto.
Fig. 243.

VIENNA, GEMÄLDEGALERIE, No. 417

St. Jerome. Single figures of St. Jerome by Tintoretto are mentioned frequently by the older writers. But there is no proof that this picture is one of these, nor that it is, in particular, the one seen by Ridolfi in Casa Priuli. It is first mentioned in Vienna in the Mecheln catalogue of 1783 as by Jacopo Tintoretto, and from Otto Mündler and Wickhoff down to the 1907 Vienna catalogue it is ascribed to Palma Giovane. The latest Vienna catalogue returns to Tintoretto and dates the picture between 1555 and 1560, as do Bercken-Mayer (I, 235) and the catalogue of the Mostra (No. 24). This dating is probably based on the stylistic relationship with the Evangelists in Santa Maria Zobenigo, Venice. Thode, on the other hand, dates it definitely about 1577. With regard to this picture it should be noted that the figure corresponds exactly, but in reverse, to one of the Philosophers in the Libreria which is held to be a product of Tintoretto's workshop. The squared drawing (No. 5660) in the Horne bequest at Florence (Tietze, Venetian Drawings, No. 1650) is a sketch for this Philosopher, though Pittaluga (p. 228) erroneously connects it with the Vienna picture. It is a typical school drawing, thus providing additional proof that the Philosopher is a workshop product. It is naturally possible that, as Wilde assumes in his report on the Mostra (Zeitschrift für Kunstgeschichte 1938, p. 140 f.), the Philosopher is derived from an original conception by Tintoretto, represented by the St. Jerome in Vienna. But against this theory we have the fact that the Philosopher with its studied attitude is in complete agreement with the rest of the series, in which the motifs become visibly more complicated, whereas the motif for a meditating saint is remarkably studied and external. The block-like vertical draperies, which form the architectural link with the niche and for which there are analogies in the rest of the series, looks as if it had been borrowed, when used for a single figure seated in the open air. The picture also lacks the spiritual concentration which we would expect from Tintoretto, for which reason the doubts expressed by scholars of previous generations seem to me justified; the reversal of a figure is quite in keeping with the habits of atelier assistants and imitators.

VIENNA, GEMÄLDEGALERIE, No. 254

Hercules driving the Faun from the bed of Omphale. 44$^{1}/_{4}$ × 41$^{3}/_{4}$. Ridolfi mentions two pictures by Tintoretto of this subject, one painted for Emperor Rudolf II and the other belonging to Nicolò Crasso, Venice. The Vienna picture is first mentioned in the Mecheln catalogue of 1783 as by Tintoretto. The new catalogue dates it about 1590. The arid treatment and the literary conception seem to me to point to Domenico.

VIENNA, GEMÄLDEGALERIE, No. 331

Mucius Scaevola before Porsenna. Originally ascribed to Tintoretto, but attributed by the 1907 catalogue and by L. Fröhlich-Bum (Jahrb. d. Kunsthist. Samml. XXXI, Plate XXV) to Schiavone; not mentioned by Hadeln, but rightly restored by Berenson and the latest catalogue to Tintoretto. The catalogue dates it about 1550—1555, but I should be inclined to say the second half of the 1550's.
Fig. 41.

VIENNA, GEMÄLDEGALERIE, No. 236

Portrait of Sebastiano Venier, the Victor of Lepanto. From the collection of the Archduke Leopold Wilhelm. Ridolfi mentions such a portrait in the Palazzo Barbarigo and another as belonging to Nicolò Crasso. Doubts as to the authenticity were first raised by Adolfo Venturi; the catalogue calls it "a later workshop replica of an original painted between 1571 and 1577" (the year of Venier's election as Doge). Recently Fiocco (Burl. Mag. LXI, 196) has tried to prove that the lifesize full-length portrait in Palazzo Mocenigo, Venice, is this original. His statements have been refuted by F. M. Kelly in the same magazine (LXII, p. 36). I have not seen the painting in Venice.

VIENNA, GEMÄLDEGALERIE, No. 235

Portrait of an Old Man with a boy. Inscribed: M. Z. or M. R. and 65 (date or age?). From the collection of the Archduke Leopold Wilhelm. The date given by the gallery catalogue, 1545 to 1548, does not agree with the style; the catalogue of the Mostra (No. 7), suggests that the figures which have emerged as the result of the recent cleaning are the second half of the date 1565. The stylistic resemblance to other portraits of the 1560's would confirm this. Apart from the question of the date, E. Tietze-Conrat (Gazette des Beaux-Arts 1934, 261 f.) has raised the question as to whether the picture—with extensive and decisive collaboration of Jacopo—might have been painted by his daughter Marietta; the hitherto unexplained initials on the picture might be those of her name (Marietta Robusti), while the older writers praise as her best work the portrait of her grandfather Marco dei Vescovi with his grandson Pietro, and there is no record of the existence of such a double portrait by Jacopo.
Fig. 153.

VIENNA, GEMÄLDEGALERIE, No. 328

Portrait of a white-bearded Old Man. 36 × 21⁷/₈. Considerably cut down at the sides. From the collection of the Archduke Leopold Wilhelm. Attributed by Wickhoff to Domenico Tintoretto, then described as "Venetian, second half of 16th century," but now assigned by the gallery catalogue to Jacopo and dated about 1570. These decisions seem to me correct and are followed by the catalogue of the Mostra (No. 53).

VIENNA, GEMÄLDEGALERIE, No. 242

Portrait of a Man. 19³/₄ × 14¹/₈. Dated by the gallery catalogue about 1555 to 1560.

VIENNA, GEMÄLDEGALERIE, No. 244

Portrait of a Man in gilded armour. 45⁵/₈ × 38⁵/₈. The age of the sitter is inscribed on the base of the pillar: XXX. Painted about 1560. Bercken-Mayer (I, 58) find here traces of the predilection for atmosphere in Venetian portrait-painting of the early Cinquecento, in contrast to Titian.

VIENNA, GEMÄLDEGALERIE, No. 250

Portrait of a Man before a table. Inscribed : MDLIII ANN XXXV. Known to have been in the gallery since 1824. Bercken-Mayer (I, 57, 258) note the prevailing lyrical, almost Giorgionesque tone of the picture.
Fig. 76.

WASHINGTON, D.C., NATIONAL GALLERY OF ART, No. 825

Christ on the Sea of Galilee. Coll. Count J. Galotti, Arthur Sachs, S. Kress. All art critics agree as to the outstanding artistic qualities of this painting, they disagree, however, vehemently as to its date, the opinions varying from Tintoretto's earliest to his latest period. Such an uncertainty where a prominent work of a prominent artist is concerned shakes the confidence in the attribution altogether. The relationship to El Greco noticed for many details by various critics and explained by an alleged influence of Tintoretto on the younger artist, may lead the way to a more satisfactory re-attribution of this great painting. Plate III (page 20).

WASHINGTON, D.C., NATIONAL GALLERY OF ART, No. 747

Portrait of a Man. 43 × 34. From the Holford Coll., London. A rather conventional portrait of c. 1570.

WASHINGTON, D.C., NATIONAL GALLERY OF ART, No. 291

The Worship of the Golden Calf. 62⁵/₈ × 107. Formerly in the Hastings Coll., England. Hardly from the latter part of Tintoretto's first period, as suggested by the catalogue ; perhaps on the contrary, because of its daring colours, late and related to Marco Tintoretto's style. Fig. 288.

WEIMAR, MUSEUM

Portrait of Jacopo Sansovino, see Florence, Uffizi, No. 957

DRAWINGS

AN ENUMERATION of Tintoretto's drawings would be superfluous here, as they are listed in H. Tietze and E. Tietze-Conrat, *The Drawings of the Venetian Painters of the XVth and XVIth Centuries* (New York 1944), where we endeavoured to distinguish critically between those made by Jacopo himself, by his children Domenico and Marietta, and by other members of his shop remaining anonymous for the time being, and perhaps for ever. Our efforts were facilitated by, and based upon, Detlev von Hadeln's book on Tintoretto's drawings (Berlin 1922), to which Hadeln himself added supplementary material in various articles. Though differing in several points from Hadeln's results we consider his book an extremely valuable piece of scholarship and a sound foundation for all further studies in this field. Our own, though forced by the nature of a catalogue to stress attributions to individual artists, in fact emphasized the rôle played by drawings within the activities of a well-manned and immensely busy shop like Tintoretto's.

For Tintoretto and his followers, drawing was a means of preparing painted compositions, a means of study and instruction, a link between the various productions of the shop, and a vehicle of their stylistic unification. The number of drawings still existing is very considerable. Our catalogue lists and describes about 200 under the name of Jacopo Tintoretto, three under that of Marietta, over 100 as shop productions in general, and about 80 as by Domenico Tintoretto, including among the latter the so-called sketchbook in London, formerly claimed for Jacopo, but now by convincing reasons ascribed to Domenico. The bulk of this mass of drawings is formed by studies after separate figures, a preparatory material of their compositions to which Jacopo and his followers attributed essential importance. Another group is formed by studies from classic and modern sculpture, again only in part by the master himself, who evidently led his pupils the same road he had found useful for himself. A third group, rather insignificant in quantity, are sketches for whole compositions executed in brush, while a certain number of pen-drawings of this character, mostly in Salzburg, formerly given to Jacopo Tintoretto, were firmly established by E. Tietze-Conrat as being by Palma Giovane.

LIST OF DRAWINGS REPRODUCED IN THIS VOLUME

BERLIN, CABINET OF ENGRAVINGS, No. 4193
Sketch for the Venus and Vulcan in the Ältere Pinakothek, Munich (Fig. 56). Pen and wash, heightened with white, on blue paper. 8×10¾. (Tietze, Venetian Drawings, No. 1561.) Fig. 55.

BERLIN, CABINET OF ENGRAVINGS, No. 5736
Study from the head of Giuliano de' Medici. Chalk, heightened with white, on greenish-blue paper. 16½×11. (Tietze, Venetian Drawings, No. 1478.) Probably by Domenico rather than by Jacopo Tintoretto. Fig. 213.

FLORENCE, UFFIZI, SANTARELLI, No. 7498
Sketch for the Return of the Prodigal Son in the Ducal Palace, Venice (Fig. 74). Charcoal on blue paper. 14⁷/₈×10¾. (Tietze, Venetian Drawings, No. 1648.) Fig. 73.

FLORENCE, UFFIZI, No. 12945
Study in the nude of a kneeling youth. Charcoal on brownish paper. 13³/₈×9⁷/₈. (Tietze, Venetian Drawings, No. 1492.) Used for the female saint below on the right in the Immaculate Conception at Stuttgart and perhaps by Domenico. Fig. 173.

FLORENCE, UFFIZI, No. 12986
Preliminary drawing for a Philosopher (Fig. 160) in the Libreria, Venice. Charcoal, slightly heightened with white, on grey paper. 11¾×7⁷/₈. Squared. (Tietze, Venetian Drawings, No. 1625.) Fig. 159.

FLORENCE, UFFIZI, No. 12929
Study in the nude for a bowman in the Capture of Zara, Ducal Palace, Venice (Fig. 236). Charcoal on brown paper. 14³/₈×8⁵/₈. Squared. (Tietze, Venetian Drawings, No. 1590.) Fig. 239.

LONDON, VICTORIA & ALBERT MUSEUM, DYCE 243
Study for a Horseman in the San Rocco Crucifixion (see folding plate). Black chalk, heightened with white, on blue paper. Squared. 12¼ × 8⁵/₈. (Hadeln, Burlington Magazine 44, p. 278, Plate I B, where the drawing is erroneously said to be an Apostle in the Last Supper in Santo Stefano [Fig. 178] ; this is now corrected in Tietze, Venetian Drawings, No. 1702.) Fig. 133.

NAPLES, PINACOTECA, No. 0193
Sketch for the Battle on the Taro, in the Gonzaga cycle, now at Munich, 1580 (Fig. 220) Brush drawing, grey, yellowish-brown and white on blue paper. 9³/₈ × 14⁷/₈. The drawing and its connection with the Munich picture were discovered by Professor Ortolani, director of the Naples gallery. (S. Tietze, Venetian Drawings, No. 1724.) Fig. 219.

PARIS, LOUVRE, No. 5384
Study from a sculpture (in the style of Michelangelo's Crepusculo). Black chalk. (Tietze, Venetian Drawings, No. 1739.) Fig. 137.

PARIS, LOUVRE, No. 5382
Study for the corpse in St. George slaying the Dragon, London (see coloured plate). Black chalk, squared. (Tietze, Venetian Drawings, No. 1738.) Fig. 65.